Making POLDARK

ROBIN·ELLIS

Robin Ellis (signature)

Palo Alto Publishing

First edition 1978
by Bossiney Books
St Teach, Bodmin Cornwall

Second edition 1987
by Crossaction Ltd
London

Third edition 2012
by Palo Alto Publishing
Palo Alto, California

Fourth edition 2015
by Palo Alto Publishing
Palo Alto, California

Book design and layout
Amy Pilkington

Publishing consultant
Holly Brady
Brady New Media Publishing

Other books by Robin Ellis
Delicious Dishes for Diabetics: A Mediterranean Way of Eating
(2011)

Healthy Eating for Life
(2014)

Softcover ISBN: 978-0-9839398-7-0
Ebook ISBN: 978-0-9839398-8-7

In remembrance of my parents
Molly & Tony Ellis
who never discouraged me
from being an actor.

Drawing by Hope James

Contents

About the Book

Ghosts frequent the publishing world. Sir Michael Parkinson, the English broadcaster and author, has likened ghosted books to "a slight snack to be eaten between meals." *Making Poldark* may be a slim publication, but every word was written in painstaking longhand by Robin Ellis. He is truly actor turned—albeit briefly—author.

The man responsible for this change of role is Cornish bookseller Bob Gilbert of Truro. It was he who told me, "Robin Ellis may have a book for you about *Poldark* inside him." One telephone call and two days later, it was agreed Robin would come to Cornwall again. This time not to act *Ross Poldark*, but to talk about the making of the *Poldark* TV series, and, to be truthful, we planned to tape those conversations for a ghosted paperback. But in the end Robin decided to write it himself.

For all followers of the series and readers of the celebrated *Poldark* novels, Robin gives us a new insight into the whole *Poldark* saga. But *Making Poldark* is more than just that. There are fragments of autobiography; there are perceptive observations on Cornwall and the Cornish way of life; and there are revealing passages on the trials and tribulations of a professional actor. A several-sided story, in fact, as you would expect from a man who swam and rode, fought and duelled for his life as *Ross Poldark*.

—*Michael Williams, 1978*

About the New Editions

*M*_{aking} *Poldark* was republished in a slightly expanded form in 1987.

The third edition was expanded to cover the "non-making" of the third series of *Poldark,* as well as the author's subsequent acting career and new ventures in healthy cooking. (*Poldark* cooks!) Two personal photo albums—one from Winston Graham, the other from the author himself, were also added.

This fourth edition includes a new chapter on the 2015 Mammoth Screen adaptation of *Poldark* in which the author played a cameo role.

About the Author

Robin Ellis is a British actor best known for playing the leading role in the BBC series, *Poldark*, based on the novels of Winston Graham. He appeared in many other classic TV series and has had a long career in British theatre, including a stint with the Royal Shakespeare Company. His most recent role was in the new Mammoth Screen adaptation of *Poldark* playing a cameo as *Dr. Halse*. He appeared in the Swedish version of the detective series, *Wallander*. He starred in the Merchant Ivory film, *The Europeans*, and can been seen in *Fawlty Towers*, *The Good Soldier*, *Blue Remembered Hills* and *Elizabeth R.*

He now lives in Southwestern France with his American wife. His life-long passion for cooking plus a diagnosis of type 2 diabetes has led to writing his first cookbook, *Delicious Dishes for Diabetics: A Mediterranean Way of Eating*, published in 2011 by Constable & Robinson in Great Britain and by Skyhorse in the United States.

His second cookbook, *Healthy Eating for Life*, was published in 2014 by Constable & Robinson in Great Britain and Palo Alto Publishing in the United States. He also leads popular healthy cooking workshops in his village of Lautrec in France.

He blogs regularly on food, cooking and life in rural France at http://robin-ellis.net, and you can follow him on Facebook and Twitter.

Getting the Part

It was a lovely sunny day, I remember, and I was going to an interview at the BBC. Another interview! I'd been to hundreds before. I'd been to three in this particular building—and I'd got all three jobs. What had my agent said? It's for a thing called *Poldark*, written by a man whose name rang a bell—Winston Graham—and set in 18th century Cornwall.

My only recollection of Cornwall was as a boy of 13 or so, being taken to Trevone by my parents on holiday. I remember playing cricket on the beach with a Welsh boy whom I instinctively disliked. He was dark-haired, bossy and dangerous, and I wanted to win. I also fell in love with a very pretty girl called Judy, so—come to think of it—my memories of Cornwall were somewhat emotional, not inappropriately.

I sat facing the sun in the producer's office, my eyes twitching, and thinking of the third degree. As always happens, he covered the awkwardness of the situation by giving me an outline of the story while looking me up and down and through and through. The subtext of first interviews is always more interesting than the scene itself. Perhaps this is what was really going on:

Producer: *He's a bit tall and maybe a bit too relaxed. What did his agent say he'd done—Essex in Elizabeth R? Well, I could have a look at that.*

"Thanks for coming in. Of course, I'm seeing others for this part....I want to get it right—but very good to meet you at last. I've wanted to use you for some time."

Me: *I feel like a monkey at the zoo. How dare they treat me like this? He must know I can act. What did he say? Twelve weeks filming in Cornwall?*

"Nice to meet you, too. Left at the end of the corridor, did you say?"

I went to a bookshop in Gloucester Road to buy the books and attacked *Ross Poldark* for the rest of the afternoon.

I went through two more of these interviews and read a scene or two for the directors. By the end of the third interview I was quite keen to get the part.

As *Captain Blood*'s wife, aged eight, middle mop cap—first part ever

I'd spent most of the previous three years with a theatre group called The Actors Company. The company had been formed in 1972 by Ian McKellen. We were a democratic company running our own shows and the responsibility for their success or failure was ours alone. People in the business had said it would never work—

actors in charge! We opened at the Edinburgh Festival to rave reviews and the next three years I traveled everywhere with them, from Liverpool to Bath and from Hull to New York. Like playing squash with someone better than you, you might lose—but you improve your game. I became a better actor.

I loved the work—Shakespeare, Chekhov, Feydeau, Congreve—classic plays in a good company. But after three years in the theatre, I wanted to do some television again—to be seen by a wider audience.

Waiting to hear whether you've got something you want is one of life's more exquisite pains—so much better than hearing that you've got it. I remember having a wonderful time pacing about my room at home, aged 15, waiting to hear whether my trial for the 1st XI Football at Highgate School had been successful. This is the most important night of my life, I remember thinking to myself. I got in—and all I could come up with was, *well, of course!*

aged 17   aged 18

After a weekend of joyful anguishing about the *Poldark* job, my agent rang and said simply, "The BBC would like you to do it and this is the offer. ...What shall I say?"

Well, of course I've got it, I thought.

"I'd like more money...."

"I'll see what I can do."

We settled and I took two bottles of champagne 'round to my agent's office. My mother and father were thrilled and probably did all the leaping about for me. I'm sure I enjoyed telling them about the jobs I got more than I actually enjoyed getting the jobs.

We were set to do the first four of Winston Graham's novels in 16 one-hour episodes between late March and early December 1975, with eight weeks of location filming in Cornwall spread throughout the year. This was the longest television job I'd ever had. I'd done three classic serials for the BBC—*The Moonstone* by Wilkie Collins, *Bel-Ami* by Guy de Maupassant, and *Sense and Sensibility* by Jane Austen—and a lot of other television work—but nothing like this.

In *Sense and Sensibility* with Clive Francis –
later *Francis* in *Poldark*, Ciaran Madden and Joanna David

And it was going to involve more than just acting.

"Can you ride?" the producer asked at that first interview.

"Yes," I said with confidence, trying to remember the last time I'd sat on a horse. I had really only ridden on television for shows like *Elizabeth R*. It made me nervous just thinking about that. I didn't tell the producer that one day, as *Essex*, I was sitting on my horse in full armor in the middle of Surrey, doubling for Ireland, with an enormous helmet on my head, and as I tried to get off, I became top-heavy and crashed to the ground.

Having got the part, and more from a powerful sense of self-preservation than belated honesty, I suggested it might be a good idea if I took a few lessons before going to Cornwall for the first two weeks of filming.

So I went off to a riding school in Manchester for a few muscle-sore days. And I'm very glad I did. When I arrived in Cornwall, I met my horse Dennis. He stood 16-and-a-half hands. What's more, he was an ex-steeplechaser and a not-yet-retired cross-country expert. In fact, without knowing it, I had watched him on television two weeks earlier at the Hickstead Easter cross-country meeting. Those were eager horses!

Dennis and I worked up a good relationship over the year. He did the riding for me and I thought I had the edge on him in the acting—until I watched one of the episodes months later and saw him smiling at the camera as we rode through. They say never act with children or animals.

Dennis threw me twice—but I was lucky. Once I landed on my feet, and once flat on my back. He loved to run and I just gritted my teeth and hung on, trying to look like one of the best riders in 18th-century Cornwall; I think he knew I was only acting. Maybe that's why he was always smiling.

So we were at the starting gate, waiting for the off. I knew these were wonderful stories and the characters were enthralling. We could be on a winner. But you can't legislate for success in this business. We had no idea how the race would run. All you can do is keep smiling—like Dennis!

Being thrown by Dennis.
The clue is the flying tricorn hat!

We Make a Start

In the UK when *Poldark* was being made, most of a television series was shot in the studio with four or five electric cameras facing the actors, like Daleks [robots], recording the show scene by scene over two days. We rehearsed for this studio work as we would rehearse for a play in the theatre.

But on location, only one camera was used. This footage was added later after the studio work was completed.

It was bitterly cold and dank on the first day's filming. We were in Towednack churchyard near St Ives. On went the first scar of many, made unromantically of glue; on went the make-up and the back-piece of hair. My hair had been dyed darker with copper tints for the part. I put on my black mourning coat—the scene was *Uncle Charles'* funeral—and my specially-made boots and there I was: *Captain Ross Poldark*.

But as the day wore on and they still didn't get to my bit, I began to wonder. I saw the director looking worried and thought at first it must be the weather. Then I thought maybe it's my hair, then my scar, then my face. Then I thought, my God, it's me! They don't want me. They think they've made a mistake! They're recasting— the lines are hot to London and actors are streaming into the producer's office and they're all Olympic equestrians.

Towednack Churchyard ... *"I remember it well."*

"Robin, will you come to the graveside please?"

Of course I've got it—I mean—of course I will. I'd started at last.

Winston Graham published the first two *Poldark* novels, *Ross Poldark* and *Demelza*, within a year of each other at the end of the war. They and the subsequent books enjoyed considerable success over the next 25 years. They are an accurate, moving picture of Cornwall in the late 18th century. They also tell a marvelous story with complex characters who push the action along with their own obsessions.

Winston and his wife, Jean, knew the region well. They'd lived in Cornwall for 28 years and brought up two children there. We, the cast, met them late on in the making of the first series—but we quickly made them part of our family.

As the books were well known long before the TV series was planned, we would obviously have something of a following, especially in the West Country; but when we started, we had no idea how popular the program would become. But we were going to have to wait until October before the series started going out to get some audience reaction. So we were working in limbo and living day to day. In fact, we had recorded nine episodes of the series before the first one was shown.

Ross Poldark. Here the tricorn hat stays on *Ross'* head....

For the location work on the first series, we were based mainly at the Carbis Bay Hotel in the next bay to St Ives. It is a great old hotel, Edwardian I imagine, just up from the beach—and we had some fair old times there.

Much of our filming was done in the area west of St Ives. In the mornings we set off on the hour's drive along the spectacular coast road to Land's End—through Zennor and Morvah to Pendeen and Botallack. It's bleak and bare shrub land with few trees—a lonely part of the world. It reminds me strongly of the southernmost tip of the Peloponnese in Greece where I once saw single olive trees guarded jealously with dry stone walls around them. In April there's a strong climatic difference, but on a hot summer's day in a brilliant light....but then you see the mine chimneys on the coast around Botallack—and you know this is Cornwall, not Greece.

Zennor

Those chimneys have tremendous power. They tell their story just by being there—the story of Cornwall—a land of great scenic beauty, scarred by the need for survival.

The tin and copper mines gave work to the Cornish for centuries—much needed work—and they left their mark. They also provided me with a feeling of continuity; a visible link with the Cornwall of the 1780s and '90s that we were trying to recapture. These reminders of another era made me feel less of a fool as I strode around this part of the peninsula in my breeches and boots.

The home of *Ross Poldark*, inherited upon his return from the war of American independence, is called Nampara. For the first series we used two houses—the back of one at Pendeen and the front of another at Botallack. *Prudie* would be doing the washing in the yard at Pendeen while *Demelza* was sitting in the front garden at Botallack—but the viewer would never know.

That front garden was beautiful—full of flowers and shrubs. I was told that on the wall surrounding it John Wesley preached his new religion. In a poverty-stricken mining community, he must have made a lot of converts—Methodist chapels abound in this area.

So much happened in that garden—the old house must have got a little confused! *Francis* fought that senseless duel with *Captain Blamey; Ross* was arrested for wrecking by a platoon of Scots Guards; *Jud* was always loping around, busy finding nothing to do.

Apart from the odd telephone wire, this garden hadn't changed much in 200 years and the atmosphere it exuded fed our imaginations and helped us create our fantasy world.

Normal hours don't exist when filming. Up at 6:30am, into costume if you can find it in the dark and down to the make-up caravan where Magdalen Gaffney, the make-up supervisor, always had the added task of trying to get the scar in the same place each time. We usually got the cheek right—but the angle was more of a problem.

Then breakfast.

Eating habits change when you're filming—at least mine did. Of course, we are working long, hard hours in the fresh Cornish air and needed the extra intake to keep going. That's what I always told myself. About 10:30am there were bacon butties and coffee; at 1pm a three-course lunch. Then at 4pm, tea and sandwiches and in the evening a dinner. And *Ross* is supposed to be a lean man!

We usually filmed until the light faded—anytime between 6pm to 8pm depending on the time of year. Then into the coach and back to the hotel for a hot bath in anticipation of the real day beginning.

After dinner until they closed the bar in the early hours we would "relax"—a euphemism for regularly drinking too much, regularly regretting it the next morning and regularly relying on the poor makeup department to repair the damage! They did their best—but they had their job cut out!

Botallack Mine

For the *Poldark* location filming, we were in Cornwall for at least two weeks each time—long enough for the crew and actors to get to know each other. We all joined in the fantasy together.

Botallack Manor Farm

Our second visit was in late May and early June and the weather was sensationally good. Apart from the 12 hour working days, it felt like being on holiday on the Continent. By this time we had completed the filming and recording of the first four episodes. They were "in the can". We had worked hard and felt it was time for a party. The middle Sunday of the two week schedule was free, so John Bloomfield, our brilliant costume designer, and Ros Ebutt, his assistant, organized a barbecue.

I'll never forget that Sunday. We were in a field in Relubbus alongside a stream. We ate and drank in the sun and the shade.

We napped for an hour—then the Cornish spirit took hold of us and we played games till the sun went down. We pole-vaulted the stream.

We tossed the caber, ran races round the field. Richard Morant, who played *Dr Enys* in the first series, is the competitive type, and as I discovered that afternoon, he liked to win. In fact, he won most of the events that afternoon.

George and *Elizabeth Warleggan* with her son,
Geoffrey Charles, and *Morwenna*

The main race was about 300 yards. Now, I fancied myself for this. After all, I'd won the 880 yards at school and that was only 15 years ago. I set off at a terrific pace. *Kill them at the start*, I thought. Kill them? I led by 10 yards with 100 yards to go. Then Richard started to close. Wily old thing, he'd been saving it. He got closer and I got whiter. With 10 yards to go he was inches behind. Now I suppose the result should be that he pipped me at the post, but actually I won by a nose—big noses come in useful now and then! I won—but at what cost? I managed a smile of condolence, shook him by the hand and collapsed on the ground. I did not rise for an hour-and-a-half.

We repaired—I use the word advisedly—to a pub in Trewellard and drank cider, singing the night away until "the gunpowder ran out at the heels of our boots". I thought we'd had a truly Cornish day.

Richard Morant did not join the cast until this period of filming. He came into the story in Episode Five. We had never met before, although I knew his work, especially his *Flashman* in *Tom Brown's Schooldays*.

Filming at Port Quin

For the wrecking scene and others in and around Port Quin, we had moved up the coast to the St Moritz Hotel in Trebetherick.

I had the afternoon off and was sitting in the sun having a cup of tea on the lawn, when up from the beach came Sheila White and Martin Fisk who were playing the ill-fated pair, *Karen Smith* and *Mark Daniel*. They told me they'd arrived that afternoon by train from London with Richard Morant who had gone upstairs for a rest. We all had tea and got to know each other, talking about lots of things including my character, *Ross*. Rather flippantly I said he was a sort of Stewart Grainger character—the hero type. Then Richard joined us, looking sleepy and a bit grumpy. Martin introduced me as Stewart Grainger and we all laughed. Richard sat down and had some tea and was very silent. I thought I sensed a certain aggressiveness towards me. I'm being paranoid, I thought. Time passed, the sun was shining, and then out of the blue he turned to me and said, "And who are you when you're not Stewart Grainger?"

I stiffened, managed a smile and said, "I'm Robin Ellis, how do you do?"

"What are you playing?" he asked.

"*Ross*."

"Ah…!" he said.

"I think I'll have a bath," I said and excused myself. An hour later we met in the bar and he bought me a pint—and we've been the best of friends every since.

Richard, Sheila and Martin had come down to do the filming around *Dwight*'s cottage, which was the extraordinary Victorian folly on the cliffs overlooking Port Quin Bay. We were all there to do the wrecking scene and the subsequent attack by the militia. "Rich pickin's for all," as *Jud* said.

Port Quin is a lovely little bay, off the beaten track and quite unspoiled. Many of the old cottages have been converted into holiday homes by the National Trust and they look very comfortable. When these are not occupied, the place is deserted.

The story of Port Quin is a famous one and has been retold by the Cornish for years. The village was once was a busy fishing port—but one night in the 19th century all the men put to sea as usual for pilchards and herring. It was stormy and the sea was rough. The women were fearful. The next morning there was no sign of their men. Days passed and still they didn't return. Distraught but resigned, the families of the fishermen gave up hope and the whole community moved to Port Isaac. Port Quin was deserted from that day to this. A tragic tale…

Ross and *Demelza*

Wrecking

A.K.Hamilton Jenkin writes in *The Cornish Miner:*
"The psychology of Cornish people towards wrecking requires perhaps a little explanation. Their attitude, being one of thankful acceptance, was long ago expressed in the localised version of the proverb: 'It is an ill wind that blows no good to Cornwall'."

The filming of the wrecking scene in *Poldark* was one of the high-spots of the series for me. Equity, the actors' union, says that outside a reasonable radius of a TV centre, television companies are at liberty to use local people as extras. So the BBC did—and what a day we all had!

A trading ship linked to the *Warleggans* had run aground on the rocks near Nampara. Word spread quickly through the nearby villages and a large crowd of hungry people gathered on the beach. Two National Trust cottages had been hired by the BBC to house the costume and make-up departments. In one door would go a steady stream of well-fed, healthy-looking local residents and out of another would come an equally steady stream of dirty, dangerous, hungry-looking 18th century Cornish wreckers. When the transformation process had finished and the obligatory coffee had been consumed, the crowd collected on the beach to await instructions from the director.

A large scaffolded platform had been built in the shallows by the camera crew for a high wide-shot from the sea. The property department waded into the sea with barrels, bits of broken timber, leather bottles and sacks.

Lizard Light "... 'depriving them of God's blessing'."

Through his megaphone, the director explained the scene: "You haven't eaten properly for weeks," he said to a lot of smiling faces. "Corn prices are high and still rising. The ship on the rocks is loaded with corn, pilchards and brandy."

"When I shout action, I want you all to rush into the water and grab anything you can find. You are mad with hunger and will soon be as drunk as lords!"

The beach hummed with excited murmurs. Cornish accents grew broader as these newly minted professionals motivated from inside. It began to feel astonishingly real.

The prop boys left their barrels and bits in the sea and cleared out of shot. The camera crew and director were ready high up on the rostrum looking down on the multitude below. We were under starters' orders.

"*Action!*" shouted the director through his megaphone and action there was. Hordes of perfectly normal 20th century men and women from all walks of life rushed into the sea shouting and screaming, seemingly out of their minds.

As the crowd surged past, they nearly took the camera position with them. The tower swayed but survived; the camera swung 'round and recorded the amazing scene beneath.

Truly there was a wrecking going on!

Rich pickins' for all!

The fighting over the spoils looked so real, I swear a lot of private scores were settled in the sea that morning. I heard one of our professional stuntmen shouting desperately to an excited Cornishman, "Here, hold on mate—it's only a *play!*"

It took at least three shouts of *"CUT!"* through the megaphone before order was restored enough for the director to announce that he wanted to do it *all over again*. And do you know—everyone was delighted!

It was a long day with many camera set-ups and much waiting around between takes. Filming can be tedious. But those marvelous extras never complained. They were there to have fun and be part of the action. Their commitment to the day's work was total.

Of course, local people were involved all the way through the filming in both series of *Poldark*. Many were Cornishmen and women but some were not. Cornwall attracts many immigrants. Being sensitive to accents, I know I heard Birmingham, London, Manchester, Glasgow and Leeds—to name but a few—coming from the mouths of many of our local extras. The 18th century brought them together as Cornishmen and women—new and old.

George Warleggan

Down the Mine

One of the most committed non-Cornish Cornishmen I met while filming the first series was Tom Bowden, captain of the King Edward Mine, attached to the Camborne School of Mines.

Tom had been a coal miner in Leicestershire for 18 years until a heart attack prevented him from carrying on. Feeling unqualified for any other work, he was desperate until he spotted an advert in the local paper for the job at Camborne. It was the answer to a prayer. Camborne had not been a working mine for over 70 years. It was not a coal mine but the principles were the same. Tom got the job and has lived in Cornwall ever since. His enthusiasm was catching. I learned a lot in two days. I had never been down a mine before and was a bit apprehensive. We climbed down ladders to a depth of about 200 feet where it was noticeably warmer than at ground level.

Tom told me that when Camborne was a working mine, they used to go down to a depth of 3,000 feet! It was hot and streaming with water. At one point he turned off all the electric lights and the only illumination came from the candles fixed onto our hats. When those were blown out, it was pitch black. You couldn't see your hand in front of your face—a chastening experience.

Underground with Tom Bowden (far left)

According to Tom, the Cornish pasty played an important part in the daily life of a Cornish miner. Now I knew something about this great local delicacy; I had been taught the subtleties of making it by a delightful lady called Elizabeth Coad. We had spent an entire morning together inside the coach that completed *Ross'* return journey from America. Up and down a cliff road we went, astonishing the people in isolated farmhouses with the appearance out of the mist of an 18th century coach, complete with passengers and coachmen. To pass the time Elizabeth explained the intricacies of pasty-making. The pasties often contained a complete meal—the meat and potato in one half and cooked apple in the other.

Elizabeth did not reveal, however, the reason for the ridge of pastry over the top of the *pasty*.

Apparently during a day's work at the tin or copper lode, a miner's fingers would become impregnated with poison from the metal. This ridge of pastry served as a kind of handle—so the miner could eat the pasty without contaminating the main course and sweet. According to Tom, the miners used to leave the ridge of their *pasties* down the mine after their shift for the ghosts of old miners—the "Knockers"—as they called them.

Cornish extras

Poldark author Winston Graham on the set with Angharad Rees (*Demelza*),
Robin Ellis (*Ross*) and Paul Curran (*Jud*)

Back in London

Early in June 1975 we returned to London to rehearse the studio work for *Demelza*, the second *Poldark* book. The summer months are an impossible time to film in Cornwall as the narrow roads are blocked by tourists.

We rehearsed at what actors fondly nicknamed the "Acton Hilton" (demolished now) in west London—a large BBC building containing 18 rehearsal rooms. Most BBC plays and variety shows in that era were rehearsed there. From the outside it looked like a non-descript high-rise block of flats. Inside, all the rooms were identical with low ceilings and poor ventilation—hardly conducive to creative work! Give me a draughty, old church hall for rehearsals any day!

For each hour-long episode of *Poldark* we had six days rehearsing, two days shooting in the studio and one day off. We rehearsed it like a short play and it was recorded that way, too, with multiple cameras.

Doesn't sound long enough to produce good work—but not impossible if the time is used well.

Ross and *Demelza*

The Rivals: Margaret Rutherford, Sir Ralph Richardson,
Marilyn Taylerson and Robin Ellis (1967)

The Company

I had never worked with most of the regular cast of *Poldark* before, with the exception of Clive Francis (*Francis Poldark*) and Ralph Bates (*George Warleggan*). Clive and I had both appeared in the BBC's *Sense and Sensibility* (1970) and Ralph was in one of my first television plays.

Angharad Rees (*Demelza*) and I had met socially a few times before *Poldark*. Jill Townsend (*Elizabeth*), an American, was new to me as was Richard Morant (*Dr. Dwight Enys*). Mary Wimbush (*Prudie*) I had heard on the radio since school days and I was familiar with Paul Curran (*Jud*) through his distinguished work at the National Theatre.

None of us knew the others very well when we started. But for some reason, the chemistry was right and it became a magical company. We saw each other socially outside rehearsal time and this agreeable, extra contact enormously helped our work together. Ralph, Angharad and Jill had families and whenever I went to call, there were children. As I was unmarried then, they became my family. Most of the offspring appeared in the show at one time or another. Linford Cazenove, Angharad's elder boy was a most versatile performer, appearing as both *Jeremy Poldark* and *Jinny Carter*'s little girl. His untimely death at age 25 in an automobile accident in 1999 was a great sadness to us all.

Angharad Rees as *Demelza*

First Critical Reactions

When we returned to Cornwall for the last time in October 1975, we still had little idea how the series was going to go over. Episode One had been shown on the first Sunday of the month and the reviews had been mixed. *The Times* was scathing, but *The Mail* liked it—and this was the pattern.

We were not downhearted. It was not, perhaps, the sort of program that critics would embrace. But what would the public make of it?

It was shown at 7:25pm on Sundays evening—a good slot—though unfortunately we clashed with *Upstairs Downstairs* by 20 minutes. This was a blow. They were a proven success and into their fourth or fifth series. We were unknown. It was going to be a struggle. So it was a good time to leave London and go back to the now-familiar locations around St Ives and the north coast of Cornwall for the last leg of the marathon. We had one book left to do: *Warleggan.*

As *George Duroy* in *Bel-Ami*, BBC TV (1971)

Problems of Adaptation

Each book had been adapted by a different writer into four hour-long episodes. Some of the results were controversial. I know, for instance, that the books' author, Winston Graham, was furious with the radical change made in the first book about how *Ross* and *Demelza* became lovers and finally married. In sharp contrast to the book, in the TV adaptation their marriage was precipitated by *Demelza* becoming pregnant.

I could see Winston's point of view. He had taken great pains to flesh out a relationship that—in those days—was socially unacceptable—a member of the gentry marrying a miner's daughter. However the producer and the adapter obviously felt that this was too slow and subtle for television. They wanted something more dramatic.

On another occasion concerning the adaptation of the second book, *Demelza*, I remember getting very hot under the collar about a particular scene that I felt had been adapted wrongly for my character. Inauspiciously, it was scene 13A. Ironically, it had been specially written to lengthen the episode. It concerned *Dwight Enys'* reaction to *Karen Daniel's* death. I was convinced that my character, *Ross*, should be taking the heat out of the situation. However the writer had me being (I thought) far too tough on him.

I went back to the book and found that Winston's original version supported *my* instincts.

It resulted in a stand-off. Richard and I and the producers, had what might diplomatically be called "a heated discussion" which went on for a week. In the end we settled for the good old English compromise and got on with the job. However, I'm sure the incident contributed to Richard Morant's decision not to return as *Dr. Enys* in the second series.

With TV director brother Peter Ellis

Cornwall in October

Cornwall in October 1975 was cold, the balmy days of June a memory. We had some important scenes to film: the burning of Trenwith; smuggling; the ill-fated elopement of *Caroline Penvenen* and *Dwight Enys*; and the final scene on the beach where *Ross* and *Demelza* decide there is a future (and the BBC start wondering too)!

This time we were based in St Ives itself, the Carbis Bay Hotel having closed for the winter. Being in town made for a pleasant change. We could shop and use the restaurants in the evening without taking taxis. St Ives out of season is delightful. It reverts to being itself. The steep hills, rising almost out of the harbor, give the rooftops a charming higgledy-piggledy look. At this time of year it's easy to understand why it became a haven for artists.

We had a night shoot to do on the first Sunday: the sacking and burning of Trenwith. The home to *Francis* and *Elizabeth Poldark* had been marvelously represented by Godolphin House—a magnificent seventeenth century manor with a farm attached.

It was a perfect size and a good cut above Nampara, which felt right for the story. It was also a versatile location. The farm buildings had been adapted for the scene at Redruth Fair when *Ross*, buying cattle at the market, came away with more than he'd bargained for (i.e. *Demelza!*).

St Ives Harbour

Some people think an actor's life is all glamour and fun. They should come to a night shoot in October! At 2am with the rain coming down nicely, unhelpful thoughts present themselves: *What am I doing here pretending to be someone else, freezing to death and shouting angry lines at Ralph Bates—who is a friend? If I were a lawyer, I'd be in bed now and much richer anyway.*

To cap it all, I had just watched a segment of Episode Two on someone's portable TV and wasn't feeling too happy about my performance.

It was a long night and technically difficult. The special effects unit had to make it look as though the house was burning down without singeing a single floorboard. Well, they did it! And from the back of the house it looked quite real. One might say the fire was the only bright spot of the night!

At 4am, as the sky was turning grey, a group of very weary, silent people had coffee and bacon butties, fell into the coach and happily headed back to St Ives.

To my surprise, during the next few days while walking around the town, I was recognized a few times. "Hi, *Ross,*" one man had said as I was going to buy my morning paper. Taken aback for a second, I looked over my shoulder expecting to see the man he had greeted—and then realized he was speaking *to me*. "Good morning," I replied, not quite knowing who I was at that moment—but secretly feeling rather pleased. It happened two or three more times and I began to think *Television is a powerful medium! I'm famous!*

The following week I had an afternoon off and went out to do some shopping and enjoy a deserted St Ives. About 4ish I stopped outside the Elizabethan tearooms and was just about to go in when I saw Donald Douglas, who was playing *Captain McNeil,* coming towards me.

"Hello Donald," I said, "Come have a cup of tea."

He looked at his watch and replied, "Actually I'd love to but I can't—I have a train to catch."

We chatted briefly, he went off and I went into the cafe. Already there were a few people inside having tea. A man at a table with three others, put his hand out as I passed and asked, "Excuse me, would you mind settling a bet for us?"

I paused, thought about my growing fame, smiled back at him and said, "Of course I will. How can I help?"

"That chap you were talking to outside. Is he an actor?"

My face didn't change. It just got a little stiff.

"*Yes,*" I said. "*He is.*"

"Thanks!" replied the man, clearly delighted at winning his wager. I sat down and bought myself a cream tea. So much for instant fame! I decided to concentrate on the filming.

I had two more important sequences to shoot: *Ross'* return from the Scilly Isles on the smuggler's boat when he is ambushed by the militia and the final scene of Series One.

The first we did at Prussia Cove and the other at Porthcurno Beach. Fine locations! The beaches in Cornwall are surrounded by menacing cliffs that create their own atmosphere and tension. They are a director's dream, except when it's raining. We had to wait two hours early one morning before we could film the last scene of all—where *Ross* and *Demelza* embrace and stand on the brink of their new future together.

Smugglers' landing – Prussia Cove

The End of the Series

Back in London we had a month to go and four episodes to record before the party-to-end-all-parties we had been promising ourselves. It had been a hard slog. As winter approached and the days grew shorter, the effort needed for the last lap grew greater. I found it increasingly difficult to learn the lines.

The news on audience figures was encouraging. They were rising steadily. It had been a slow start. Just over five million people watched the first episode and it took some time before we had a substantial share of the early Sunday night audience. But at least we were in the market; the product we'd worked on in isolation for so long was beginning to sell.

It's a strange experience watching oneself on television. It's unreal, a totally subjective exercise. One never sees oneself performing on the stage. Most performances evaporate into thin air—and sometimes one is thankful for that. But on television it's thrown straight back at you. I find it impossible to follow the story as I spend the whole agonizing hour looking at what my arms and legs are doing. Mannerisms glare out at me—familiar and familial: I see my father lowering himself into a chair, a brother running down the road. Why do I watch? Why put myself through it?

On Tintagel cliffs

Some people say it's good to watch yourself. You see what you're doing wrong and ensure you don't repeat it. I suppose that's true but to be honest I watch because I can't resist. Sometimes it depresses me for days. I keep telling myself *Never again!* but come the night....

For months I had been in the novel position of being in near-permanent employment. During the last month I began to think about what I should do next.

I once heard Dame Edith Evans say that for her one of the most exciting times for an actor was being *out* of work. That may sound strange, but I know what she meant. Who knows what might turn up? It could be repertory theatre in the sticks for a special week or it might be a call from *Cecil B. DeMille* in Hollywood.

I do get restless. I need change—it's one of the reasons I'm an actor I suppose—itchy feet.

Midway through November, the Royal Shakespeare Company made an inquiry about my availability—and my heart sank. Back in 1964 when I left Cambridge, I could have gone to Stratford playing small parts and walk-ons. But I'd decided then that, prestigious though the Company is, it would be wiser for me—who had never been to drama school—to go into repertory theatre and learn the trade by *doing* it, rather than by watching the famous do it.

So I had gone to Salisbury for 18 months, played everything from *Olde Tyme Music Hall* to *Shakespeare*—and had the happiest time of my life.

I'd heard from a number of people over the years how badly actors were treated at Stratford—and that hadn't encouraged me to try again. Anyway, I'd been a founder-member of the groundbreaking Actors Company, where we took all the artistic decisions ourselves, so the thought of becoming a cog in the wheels of an enormous company was not attractive. Nevertheless I went to see them and the offer they made was good—but I turned it down. My fellow actors thought I was crazy—but I was adamant. I didn't want to spend a whole year in the country playing Shakespeare.

Looking back I think I was a bit scared. Deep down under all those excuses, nagging away at my ambitious, romantic soul, was the feeling that maybe there was a film out there. Maybe I was going to be snapped up for some starring role. *Ready when you are, Mr. DeMille*, I thought.

At Land's End cottage

We finished the series with a bang—in fact, we nearly burned down the BBC Television Centre. The last scene to be done in the studio was the burning of Trenwith—from the inside. This was another diversion from the books where Trenwith is kept intact by author Winston Graham.

For television a more dramatic climax was needed, and what better than disaffected and starving miners torching the boss' home?

The set was a fine recreation of an 18th century upper-class living room filled with a mixture of real antiques, good reproduction furniture and *objets d'art*—well in line with the BBC tradition of authenticity. It had cost a fair amount to put together.

As the scene begins, *Ross* tries to persuade a stubborn *George Warleggan* and his wife *Elizabeth* to run for their lives. *Demelza* arrives with news that the attack is imminent, and an angry mob of miners burst in.

The miners, professional extras, had been given instructions to set light to the place with their burning torches. This they did with great enthusiasm. Original 18th century furniture was smashed and burned. But nobody shouted *"CUT!"* so this bizarre spectacle continued rather longer than necessary—prompting an enquiry later!

For the actors, it was a spectacular ending to an eventful nine months. Exhausted, we trooped off to the much anticipated wrap party at Angharad's house—and it was not a disappointment. Two hundred of us celebrated until eight the next morning. Thus the curtain came down on the making of the first series of *Poldark*. I had made many new friends. I'd spent two months in the open air, in a most beautiful part of the country and got paid for doing it. It had been a wonderful time that I shall always look back on with affection and warmth.

And that was a general feeling. Whatever the shortcomings and frustrations of doing television, we had enjoyed ourselves. Maybe that's putting it too mildly—we'd had a ball. And now it was a sweet luxury having nothing to do but sit back and wait for Christmas.

After the festivities the Royal Shakespeare Company came back and made an even *better* offer, damn them! My agent played the heavy father and being less tired, I saw reason, buried my prejudices and plumped for a year in the country at Stratford-on-Avon. I shall never regret it.

As a sulking *Achilles* in *Troilus and Cressida*, Stratford-on-Avon (1976)

At Stratford with the RSC

My first part was *Don Pedro* in *Much Ado About Nothing* with Judi Dench and Donald Sinden as *Beatrice* and *Benedick,* directed by John Barton. We were to rehearse for 12 weeks—the same time it took to do eight episodes of *Poldark!* We were in London for 10 weeks and went to Stratford in the middle of March.

I'd been to Stratford as a stage-struck schoolboy in 1959 for the centenary season. I'd see Paul Robeson as *Othello,* Laurence Olivier as *Coriolanus* and Charles Laughton as *Lear.* Later, in 1962, I'd slept outside the theatre to get standing tickets for the magnificent production of the *Wars of the Roses* that this very same John Barton had done with Peter Hall.

So when I walked on to the Stratford stage for the first time, it felt a little unreal. There were ghosts around and I could not quite believe that in two weeks time I'd be joining the cast out there in front of 1,500 people.

I rented a cottage in the village of Snitterfield, four miles outside Stratford, where Shakespeare's father once lived. Mine being a 16th century cottage and me being a romantic, I quickly convinced myself that they'd got the birthplace wrong and William had in truth been born in my bedroom. I decided against proving my case when I realized I might have five million unwelcome visitors during the year.

I'd never lived in the country. I was a townie born and bred—and it was a revelation to me. That year, 1976, was famous for its summer. It was so hot the English character *changed*—I swear it. We were no longer the phlegmatic, inhibited, unemotional lot we'd been since Victoria came to the throne and the middle classes reigned supreme. We became a nation of languid, slow moving, easygoing southern Europeans! It was wonderful to behold and a great year to spend in the countryside.

I saw all four seasons as I'd never seen them before. I'd met a lovely young actress in the Company. She lived on Dover's Hill outside Chipping Campden, and from her cottage there was a breathtaking view over the Vale of Evesham.

I played no heroes that year. I was in four productions: after *Much Ado* I played *Achilles*, a pathological killer, in *Troilus and Cressida;* then *Dr. Pinch*, a ridiculously drunk counterfeit conjurer, in the musical version of *The Comedy of Errors;* and lastly that marvelous villain, *Edmund*, the bastard son, in *King Lear*.

My fears about joining the company were not confirmed and I found Shakespeare rewarding work. It is difficult to believe that the plays were written 400 years earlier, the ideas seem so modern. I felt rejuvenated and was reminded again why I became an actor. For me, at that time in my life, there was nothing to beat live theatre at its best.

Poldark had finished its run on television two months before I arrived in Stratford—yet it was only there that its popularity got through to me. Very few people recognized me in Kensington. I concluded they'd all been watching *Upstairs Downstairs*. But in Stratford everyone seemed to have watched *Poldark*.

I discovered there were certain advantages to being well known. One traffic warden in particular was very understanding. Everyone asked, "Is there going to be another series?" For the first few months I said *"No!"*. Then I began to hear rumblings....

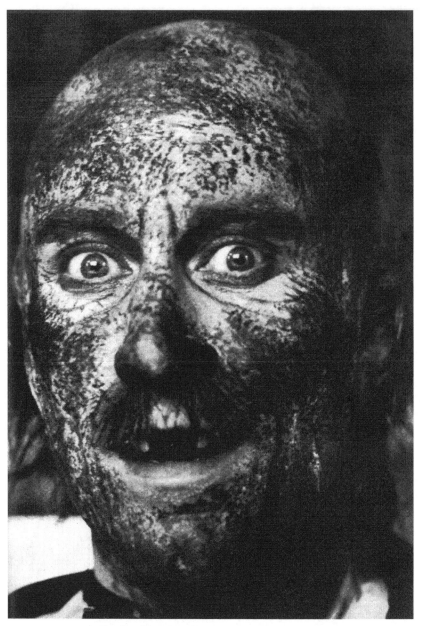

As *Dr. Pinch* in *Comedy of Errors*, Stratford (1976)

The viewing figures towards the end rose to around 12 million and the BBC were interested in a second series. There were two more books that hadn't been serialized and Winston Graham had been asked to write a third. The material was there—but did we want to do another? At the end of the first series we'd thought that was enough. It had worked once. Could it work again?

There was to be a new producer, Tony Coburn, and Winston, whom we all knew by now, was to be much more closely involved. He had had an unhappy relationship with the BBC on the first series and we were all keen that this should be put right.

Tony came to see me at Stratford in November '76.

Rehearsals, he said, would start in March '77. The three books would be done in 13 episodes and the job would run until November.

"We can't do it without *you*," he said, the old silver-tongue.

By March I would have been with the RSC 14 months. As usual the plan was to take all that season's productions from Stratford to London and run them through 1977. It was a difficult choice. To appear in London with this great company would do me no harm; on the other hand, I had done all the productions for some time and I wondered whether I could sustain an interest in them for much longer.

Silver-tongue won—and for better or worse—I decided to leave the company in March. The parts were recast and the new arrivals rehearsed into the productions. I'm not sure Trevor Nunn ever forgave me the extra work involved.

Poldark II

The only major cast change in the second series was *Dwight Enys*. Richard Morant did not want to do it again and Michael Cadman, whom I had known in the National Youth Theatre years before, took over.

After a holiday in Florence, I arrived once again at the Acton Hilton for *Poldark* rehearsals, with a distinct feeling of *déjà vu*. All the old faces were there, two years older—plus a few new ones.

We put two episodes in the can, this time at Pebble Mill in Birmingham, and left for Cornwall for six weeks filming. *How am I going to survive six weeks of fantasy?* I wondered. *The two week stints of the first series nearly killed me last time....*

For Series Two we used locations further east. Nampara had miraculously taken wing to a place further up the coast close to Port Quin, and Penrice, the new *Warleggan* stronghold, was to be represented by the Boconnoc Estate. To make these places accessible the BBC descended on the Carotel Motel at Lostwithiel, which became our base for the six weeks.

Dr. Dwight Enys, Michael Cadman

Caroline Penvenen, Judy Geeson

Return to Cornwall

Since the first series had been shown twice on television, it had a predictably large and enthusiastic following in Cornwall. Thus, there was a considerable welcoming party of young autograph hunters to greet us when we arrived at the Carotel. This was to become the rule. In each location our supporters were out in force; filming began to feel like open air theatre! It was good to be back in Cornwall.

The farmhouse at Roscarrock that was used for Nampara is half a mile or so inland and looks towards Port Quin Bay. From there one can see the Victorian folly used in the first series as *Dr Enys*'s cottage high on the cliff edge in the distance. From the novels it was exactly how I had imagined the geographical relationship. The house and the farmyard also fitted what had been in my mind's eye. For me *this was Nampara*. Uncannily so.

Like Godolphin in the first series, this too was a versatile location. It served many purposes and I grew to love it. Some parts of it are ancient—attached to the house is a 7th century chapel and the remnants of a remote and lonely monastery.

The peace and quiet associated with this site continue to inform the place—though it was rudely interrupted on many occasions by the arrival of the players!

As *Essex* with Glenda Jackson in *Elizabeth R*, the BBC TV series

There is a long high wall that protects the farmhouse from the seaward side. This became the exterior wall of a French prison, and the place where *Ross* faced the firing squad on his first expedition to France.

That clear, cold morning, the place was swarming with "French soldiers"—mostly recruited from the Wadebridge area. They were there to shoot a bedraggled chained line of defeated *aristos* (also from Wadebridge!).

Two hundred yards away there was a gate into the pasture beyond. Through this gate, in a small coach, *Ross'* rescuer would come in the shape of David McKail playing an English merchant who'd bought off the French authorities.

A camera tower, similar to the one used for the Port Quin wrecking scene, was built for the long shot. The first hour's work was pleasant in the sun, but after coffee it clouded over and the condemned men agreed that even if we weren't really going to be shot, we'd probably freeze to death anyway.

I never feel comfortable in execution scenes. My imagination works overtime. I remember being very nervous in *Elizabeth R,* filming the beheading of *Essex*. When the director shouted "CUT!"

as the executioner raised his axe over my bowed head, I nearly fainted.

But in this case, the cold froze all our imaginations and we spent the time between takes jumping up and down trying to get our circulation back. Bill Gane and his wife, the tenants of the farmhouse, brought me back to life at lunchtime with tots of whisky and a big log fire in the kitchen.

The weather improved after lunch and by the time we reached the rescue section the sun was out. The camera crew went up the tower for the long shot of the coach coming through the gate. The horse master, Ben Ford, was up in front ready to drive, and David McKail was seated comfortably inside.

Waiting for the firing squad

"ACTION!" shouted Philip Dudley, the director, and Ben took off. We watched in amazement as this whirlwind headed down the lane towards the narrow gateposts. He was not, as they say, "hanging about". He shot through the gate almost sideways and on towards the tower, missing it by inches. The camera crew, staying astonishingly cool, captured our reactions which were *right*—but for completely the *wrong* reasons. As the coach came back towards us, the door opened and David McKail, pale and shaking, shouted *"bring me a pair of brown trousers!"*. Nobody was cold again that day!

Fair scene

Rescuing Dwight Enys

This six-week period of location filming included a major sequence which took over a fortnight to complete. In television time it comprised nearly a whole episode. There was the expedition to France, the storming of Fort Baton and the rescue of *Dr. Enys* from his French prison. *Ross* couldn't resist playing the hero!

We filmed this in three locations: up the Fowey estuary at Lerryn, at sea and at St Mawes Castle. Robin and his merry men had some fun!

Lerryn as France

We were six: Peter Diamond, Forbes Collins, Terence Edmonds, Duncan Lamont, Kevin McNally and me. And these six, together with the whole mad circus of make-up, costume, props, scenic design, cameras and the director went to sea in a "pea-green boat" for the first of two days filming.

It was overcast as we left Fowey Harbor and the sea looked unfriendly. I have respect for the sea—especially 'round the Cornish coastline. As soon as we hit the open Channel it started to roll. Whether one is seasick or not is a matter of luck—sea legs are usually an accident of birth. That day we had a high proportion of people without "the luck". We were decimated. Even some of the ship's crew suffered.

For once the catering department was not overtaxed. Some of the actors decided to "use" the experience—some had no choice. Method actors were two a penny that day!

At one point there were so many bodies lying around, it looked like a hospital ship—but there was no cure except dry land. Worse, we had the prospect of repeating the experience the next day—but fortunately the sea was kinder. Even so, I prefer riding horses!

If you take the second right up the Fowey estuary, you are heading for Lerryn Creek. This particular stretch of water is one of the most beautiful I have ever seen. It's wide with heavily wooded banks on both sides. In the late afternoon the setting sun has a stunning effect on the trees, turning them silver-green. We spent what seemed like a lifetime in this area, filming the landing and escape from France.

Action sequences are intended to look exciting, but piecing them together bit by bit, day by day, is quite the opposite. It's a long, tedious business. An actor's lifeblood is *words*—and there are few in action sequences except the odd *"Over here all of you!"*, *"Keep your heads down!"*, *"Which way did they go?"* and *"We'll take the right fork—follow me, men!"*

I remember standing on a small bridge in the heart of nowhere, frantically beckoning the others to me and whispering urgently: *"Remember this bridge, it's a landmark for our return."* My merry men kept wonderfully straight faces and played the game!

It rained a lot that week and as we tramped through the wet undergrowth, the smell of wild garlic was all around us.

Two scars! – Kevin McNally getting in on the act.

The most enjoyable time was the three days we spent huddled together in a small rowing boat in the estuary. There was a definite feeling of anarchy! Being in a small boat in sheltered water was entirely different from being tossed about on the open sea!

Again the sequence took a long time to piece together. For the long shot the camera would be on the shore, then in a support boat and eventually—for the dialogue—in the boat with us. This last was very cramped—a cameraman, soundman, director and the actors in this tiny boat. We got to know each other well!

Several locations were considered for Fort Baton, the French prison where *Dwight* was being held. Finally St Mawes Castle was chosen. When we arrived by coach on the first afternoon, crowds of early holiday-makers were there to greet us. It was a stunning day and the bay looked beautiful in a shimmering light.

It was extraordinary that afternoon to turn away from the heavy industrial landscape of the 20th century in Falmouth Harbor to the lawns outside St Mawes Castle where 18th century prison gangs were hard at work putting up defenses—heavily guarded by soldiers of the new French Republic (mainly recruited from Wadebridge again).

This was the scene that *Ross* saw through his telescope on his first visit to France when he confirms that *Dwight* is indeed a prisoner and still alive.

The attack and escape and would take three long night-shoots to accomplish. By the end, we felt we really had been to France and back! The sequence ends with *Ross* riding home alone to Nampara, tired but triumphant, having engineered *Dwight* and *Caroline*'s reunion.

We filmed in a field close to Nampara. I was to ride up to camera, some 300 yards, stop, look towards my home and shout *"Demelza!"* at the top of my voice, then ride out of shot. Good romantic stuff and not too difficult, you'd think, as long as I could remain in the saddle. What we had *not* bargained for was the herd of cattle quietly grazing at the bottom of the field.

Luggers at Port Quin

The director waved to me and I started galloping up the hill. *More fun than grazing*, thought the cows and joined in. The faster I went, the faster they went. Soon I was leading a stampede and I was terrified.

Back down the field we went, *Ross* and his new band of merry men. The same thing happened. Everyone enjoyed it—the camera crew, the director, my horse and the cows—all except me. I was convinced they were going to charge my horse and I'd be thrown unceremoniously into the air. However, after three attempts, the cows decided filming was a tedious business and went back to grazing. I climbed into the Land Rover, no longer sure about my ambition to appear in a Western.

Ebony the Horse

My horse for the second series, Ebony, was supplied by the wonderful horsemaster, Ben Ford. I had more riding to do in this series, so Ebony and I saw a lot of each other. She never threw me like Dennis, but I'm sure she knew she had a novice aboard. Our most difficult day was the first shot of the series—my return from Holland.

In real life, I had been in London the previous day to see my girlfriend play *Cordelia* at the opening night of the RSC's production of *King Lear*, which had transferred from Stratford to the Aldwych Theatre. After the performance I caught the overnight train to Cornwall. So I was there, fresh as a wilted daisy, at 8am on the beach at Caerhays ready to film. It was pouring with rain. Ebony and I waited until 3:30pm before we could even get on the beach. Neither of us was in very good shape. The wind was blowing the sea into a frenzy and I had great difficulty in keeping my over-large hat on my head.

Ebony, quite sensibly, was none too keen on the conditions. She could see the waves out of the corner of her eye and thought they were coming for her. With difficulty, trying to control my hat, my flowing cloak and the reins, I managed to get her facing the right way. The camera was mounted on the roof of a Land Rover and we were supposed to follow it at full gallop across the beach.

It should have been an invigorating experience. Instead it was a nightmare. Ebony hated the sound of the Land Rover and decided the safest place was her horsebox—so that's where we headed. We passed the Land Rover with ease and I managed to stop her only a few feet from the end of the beach. Exhausted I fell off into a puddle! I remounted. (*Well, I was the hero!*)

Lunch with Winston Graham and the props department at Boconnoc

Ben, experienced in such things, placed a sister horse on the seaward side of the Land Rover track, hoping Ebony would run towards her. We tried again and Ebony rejoined her friend rather more quickly than the cameraman anticipated.

By this time, I was losing confidence and my fingers were losing their grip. We tried once more. Ebony did an impromptu gavotte, crisscrossing the Land Rover, and then another mad gallop. I decided she'd won the day and walked back to the coach.

Two days later we had a perfect sunny day and managed the shot in one take. I think Ebony had worked in television before.

Winston Graham and his wife Jean were with us throughout the location filming of the second series. They'd taken a house in Cornwall for the duration. They say they enjoyed the experience; the feeling was mutual. We'd got to know them in the interval between the first and second series and it was a bonus to have them on location. They were a source of constant support and encouragement. They both made appearances: Winston as a member of the gentry at *Drake Carne*'s wedding and Jean as a starving peasant in the scene where *John Hoskins* is arrested by *Ross*.

Trerice, now owned by the National Trust, was Winston Graham's inspiration for Trenwith, the *Warleggan* home.

Winston had helped the BBC find many of the beautiful locations. Not only had he lived in Cornwall for many years, but he was, after all, the original author and obviously had specific places in mind when writing the books. For instance, he told me that Roscarrock had been one of two places he thought of when describing Nampara. Trevellas Porth near St Agnes, another superb location that can't have changed in 200 years, was also Winston's suggestion.

About the people in the story he is more reticent. The *Warleggans* are based on two old Cornish families, but he won't say which. *Ross* is a composite of a number of men he has known.

One major location that was entirely new to him, however, was Boconnoc, the *Warleggan* home in the second series. I remember having an immediate emotional response to the Boconnoc Estate. I did not like it. There it was, all 8,000 beautiful acres of it stretching as far as the eye could see—a landscaped paradise full of trees and flowers, leafy glades and ponds. But for me, it seemed to symbolize the enormous gap between rich and poor in 18th and 19th century Cornwall.

Nevertheless, like Roscarrock and Godolphin, it was another versatile location and one Sunday provided the setting for the most extraordinary and bizarre cricket match.

Filming at Boconnoc

Poldark v Warleggan

As mentioned at the outset, I played cricket once before in Cornwall. Once again my opponent was to be a dark and dangerous man—only this time it was Ralph Bates—and he was no Welsh Ogre!

POLDARK XI v WARLEGGAN XI at Boconnoc Cricket Club the posters read. Posters, teams, a ground to play on, a date set—it all seemed so well organized. We thought we might attract a few hundred spectators if the weather was fine. We were due to start at three in the afternoon.

When we arrived at the grounds, I couldn't believe my eyes. The crowd was estimated at about 6,000 and they were still pouring in. The police opened all the gates to the estate to relieve the pressure on the main road. I ran for the pavilion where I found Ralph looking worried.

"Who is going to play for whom?"

"We'll have to start soon or they'll burn down the pavilion!"

Our nonchalant attitude towards the game during the week evaporated in two minutes at the ground. We knew that the hordes outside were going to want to see some action soon!

I sometimes have nightmares in which I'm in the theatre on opening night and realize with horror that I don't know the words. That same feeling of inadequacy was creeping up on me now. A quick look at all the familiar faces in the pavilion reassured us that at least we'd have enough players for a fielding side and two batsmen. We prayed that some of the crew had been held up and would turn up as promised. The weather, thank heavens, was fantastic, and the crowds seemed happy enjoying the sunshine.

Robin at bat

By half past three, we were ready to start. It was a relief to get onto the pitch. It was the safest place to be—the crowd had grown so huge around the pavilion.

The game was a riot and bore as little resemblance to cricket as a winged bat does to a cricket bat. Nobody seemed to care. Ralph and I tried to impose a serious tone—remembering those heady days in the 1st XI at school. But it was no good—we couldn't stop the carnival.

Elizabeth bowled *Ross* underarm—which I thought was typical of the *Warleggan* side's general underhanded tactics. Ralph eventually conceded defeat to everyone's delight—except a few rowdy *Warleggan* supporters. We all nearly died in the crush as we came off the field.

Apart from being a rather dubious cricket match on a beautiful summer's day, it was a good piece of open-air theatre, Roman circus almost. We all felt like triumphant gladiators by the end. In a way the throng had given us the thumbs up.

Back to London

Two weeks later we were back in London for a large chunk of studio work. It was good to be back home for a while. I had barely seen London for over a year. Most of 1976 had been spent in Stratford with the Royal Shakespeare Company, followed by a season in Newcastle. Then there was the six-week filming bonanza in Cornwall in 1977.

For two months that summer we had a regular routine of two weeks rehearsal in London, then up to Birmingham for two days recording. Apart from a brief visit to Gloucestershire, we didn't film again until we went to Cornwall in the autumn.

With Nicola Pagett in *Widowers' Houses* by G.B. Shaw
at the Royal Court Theatre

Whistle-Stop Tour of America

This more settled period of work was broken by one mad hiccup for Angharad and me. We were invited to go to America for a five-day whirlwind tour of four cities to promote the series. The only possible gap we could see was between recording Episodes Seven and Eight—and even then it would involve missing two days of rehearsal. Fortunately, the eighth episode was a light one for both of us and Roger Jenkins, who was directing, reorganized the schedule with great generosity of spirit to give us the two extra days off.

I left Birmingham at 10pm on Monday night having finished the seventh episode, drove at full speed to London, packed hurriedly, and tried to get a few hours sleep before the 11am flight from Heathrow the following morning.

I had been to New York City once before in 1974 with the Actors Company for a five week season at the Brooklyn Academy of Music.

The British reaction to the city is, in my experience, uncomplicated. They either love it or hate it. I *loved* it—New York was simply the most exciting place I had ever seen.

As *Theodore* in *The Wood Demon*, The Actors Company (1974)

As *Redillon* in *Ruling the Roost*, The Actors Company (1973)

The view of Manhattan Island from atop the Empire State Building is a man-made miracle! It was wonderful to be there and frustrating to leave 24 hours later.

Wednesday night we stayed at the notorious Watergate Hotel in Washington D.C. My room overlooked the Potomac River and to the right was the building that had housed the Democratic National Committee Headquarters. That feeling that had haunted me at Stratford returned here—I felt surrounded by ghosts.

After a flurry of interviews and television appearances and a quick tour of the White House, it was back to the airport and a flight to Boston. If this is Thursday, it must be Massachusetts!

As we sped by limousine towards this old Colonial town, the folks back home were assembling at the Acton Hilton for the read-through of the eighth episode. Angharad and I pinched ourselves and braced for a frenetic 24 hours of interviews.

The last stop was Dallas, Texas, and the maddest of them all. It was hot—95° F in the shade. Suddenly I was back in the summer of '76 in Stratford.

We met 300 Texans at a reception on Friday evening and then escaped to a local rodeo. All the men in Texas seemed to wear cowboy boots—so next day I bought myself a pair and thought of my *Poldark* horse, Ebony.

On Saturday, our final day in America, we went to two parties, stayed up all night, dragged ourselves to the airport at 6am and flew to Washington D.C., where we boarded Concorde—yes Concorde—and flew home at twice the speed of sound. After the previous five days this did not seem unusual.

At 10am on Monday morning we started work on Episode Eight feeling like a couple of cartoon characters who'd been hit on the head with a mallet—we were seeing stars and stripes. Two weeks later we were back in Cornwall on what felt like a holiday.

Demelza with her two brothers, *Drake* and *Sam* played by Kevin McNally and David Delve. The actresses found riding side-saddle a challenge.

The Final Hurdle

It was now September and we were nearing the end of this marathon. I had played *Ross* in 25 episodes of *Poldark*, and he was at least 12 years older than he'd been on that first wet and windy day in Towednack churchyard. He'd started life in the series as an impoverished member of the gentry with an instinctive contempt for their values and their dealings with working people. To his social peers he was a rebel, an uncomfortably disruptive force against the *status quo*. They would do their damndest to be rid of him. At the same time, he was romantically involved with two women.

So for the run of the first series, the first four books, he had his hands full. Morning, noon and night, there was drama in his life. If it wasn't father *Warleggan* threatening to ruin him, it was *Demelza* threatening to leave him. If it wasn't a false dawn at the mine, it was a false dawn at Trenwith and some days it was all four at once. All this was great fun to play. I looked forward to each episode— there's nothing like a good disaster to keep you fresh!

After 25 episodes and six books, *Ross* had come a long way. He was a Member of Parliament and a comparatively rich man. He was committed to a growing family and—apart from a few ups and downs—to his beautiful wife.

He would never stoop to being a member of the Establishment—a commendable flaw in his personality would guarantee that, but success had undoubtedly got him in its grasp. And maybe there's something essentially dull about success—at least in dramatic terms, *arrival* is not as exciting as the journey.

Ross' duel with *Captain Adderley* (Malcolm Tierney)

Given the opportunity, *Ross* was no less impulsive in his day-to-day life and sometimes still as irresponsible. He was prepared to risk his life and his family's livelihood to rescue *Dwight Enys*. And in the scene we were about to film at Boconnoc on a chilly September morning, he showed the old *Ross*—risking everything by allowing himself to be provoked into a duel with *Monk Adderley*.

If the second series was not as engrossing—in acting terms—as the first, it was no less enjoyable. The magic was there again in the Company and in a way it was more remarkable because it was a bigger regular cast of actors.

I remember a day in June during the last week of filming. Some of us had the day off and went for a picnic on the beach at

Polzeath. The sand was damp, so we bought some cheap deck chairs which started us thinking. Television filming can be very uncomfortable. The BBC, unlike the old film companies, never provides the actors with anything to sit on while they await their scene; so ladies in long tight dresses have to lie on the grass!

The next day most of the regulars were called for the filming of Sawle Feast and we knew from experience it was going to involve a lot of waiting around.

"Why don't we all arrive with our own deck chairs and stage a sit-down protest?" someone suggested. We went back and bought every chair in the shop!

As the sun shone down on the field at Roscarrock the next morning, 12 smug and smiling actors sat round in a large circle of personally marked deck chairs awaiting their call.

The happy chemistry of both casts led to many such moments of spontaneous combustion. It was a good feeling to be part of that engine.

Sawle Feast – *Ross* and *Demelza* with *Caroline* and *Drake*

Drake and *Morwenna*, Kevin McNally and Jane Wymark

The Last Shoot

The last scene I filmed in Cornwall for *Poldark* was fittingly with my beloved and talented acting partner, Angharad Rees.

She'd been wonderful to work with from the start and had kept me sane on many occasions when I thought the pressures and frustrations of the work were about to send me 'round the bend.

It was a bumpy ride by Land Rover from our base to the location high on the cliffs overlooking Port Quin Bay. Not for the first time we tinkered with the script on the journey until the words felt right and in character. Then we spent two hours on a sunny afternoon building the three-minute scene, shot by shot.

When we'd finished, it wasn't champagne all 'round and a big party, because we still had four episodes to rehearse and record back in London and Birmingham. Nonetheless, it felt the end of something. It couldn't have been a more spectacular place to finish our filming relationship with Cornwall, with the sea far below saying goodbye with great gasps of spray and the rocks staying stony-faced. I left that evening and drove back to London for the last time.

As *Ross Poldark* in the famous breeches and boots,
surveying the Cornish coastline from a rocky promontory

Six weeks later it was all over. In all we'd taken 18 months to do
29 episodes and seven books. Hilda, who worked in the restaurant
at the Acton Hilton, couldn't quite believe we were leaving.

"Aren't you going to do any more then?"

"No, Hilda, no more. That's it."

Cornish Epilogue

Soon after we'd finished filming the expedition to France, it was May Day and a group of us decided to go to Padstow for the Festival. We arrived at about 7pm and walked down the hill from the car park into the town. From far away we could hear the beat of the drums and the music. We rounded the bend and came into a square and there it was! The umpteenth parade of the hobbyhorse in full swing. The drumbeat was mesmeric and the man inside the hobbyhorse never stopped moving—round and round he went, tempting and teasing the circle of young maidens. A pagan ritual full of fun and danger. Not English at all!

All this had been going on for at least 12 hours and the atmosphere in the town was jolly—to say the least. We watched for a while and then I was recognized by someone in the crowd. George Collins, my dresser, insisted I was his cousin Fred and not *Poldark*—but he didn't convince them, so we moved on quickly to a pub down the hill.

The beer and the cider were flowing freely and not about to run out. "Cousin Fred" was recognized again and on we went. In pub after pub it happened again and again. I was bought pasties and pints everywhere and for the first time in my life I realized what it must have been like being Ringo Starr or John Lennon. A man in one of the pubs came up to me and said, "You've put Cornwall on the map. Thank you." I was amazed, flattered, a little embarrassed, and—to be honest—by this time a bit stewed.

We found a Blue 'Oss pub and settled down in a corner to listen to the man playing the accordion. We sang and danced and everyone forgot about *Poldark*. It was a great night.

I suppose I was naive to think I could go to a big Cornish festival like this and remain anonymous. Television is a powerful and popular medium, but as to putting Cornwall on the map—on the evidence of this particular evening—it occurred to me later (not at the time, you understand) that it might be the other way around!

Poldark cast and crew at Pebble Mill Studios in Birmingham

Poldark Perks

Twenty-nine hours of the life and times of the *Poldarks* of Cornwall—and that was it—up to a point. We did not shoot another frame or don another period costume (well, actually, I did—briefly, but more of that later).

A lot of people thought we were crazy. Why give up a good thing—why throw away a meal ticket (and now you know about eating on location). The answer was simple—we had told our tale, and unless it was to become the everyday story of olden Cornish folk, there was no more to be done.

Winston Graham has gone on to write about another generation of *Poldarks* and the new books have proved as hugely popular as their predecessors—but the love triangle of *Ross*, *Elizabeth* and *Demelza* was resolved.

Life after *Poldark*, however, was not to be the same as life before *Poldark*. I'm calling this chapter "*Poldark* Perks" because it's the story of how *Poldark* turned up trumps, landed me on my feet and has generally done well by me the last 10 years. I suppose it's a long-winded *thank you* to that Cornish gent—*Ross Poldark*.

The series has been sold to over 40 countries, so it's a good bet that *Ross* is probably the most prolific 18th century foreign language speaker the world has ever known.

Actors get a fee for these foreign sales, but the percentage varies enormously—something to do with the size of the market in question. This produces some extraordinary figures. The lowest aggregate I have received so far was from El Salvador for 16 hours television: £25.60.

But I'm not complaining—it was very surprising, for instance, to have two students come up to me in Florence and say how much they'd enjoyed watching *Poldark* in Israel. I have been recognized at the top of the tallest building in the world, the Sears Tower in Chicago, and waved at from a passing car on a Spanish motorway. Somebody approached me in an Italian delicatessen in New York to say what a privilege it was to have me in their shop—as every Sunday night they made a point of never missing an episode of *Dr. Who!*

Apart from the confusion with *Dr. Who*, the common factor in these encounters is a tremendous feeling of warmth towards *Poldark*. People from all over the world have an affection for this series, which is very gratifying.

The buggy ride with Lee Remick in *The Europeans*

Because of its popularity in America, I became known to American casting directors, and one recommended me to Ismail Merchant for a leading role in *The Europeans*. He and James Ivory were looking for someone to play a successful 19th century Bostonian merchant in a film of Henry James' novel.

It seemed a long shot to me. I admire American film actors—they manage a remarkable relaxation in front of a camera—surely *Robert Acton* was a part for American talent.

Over a plate of apple pie, Ismail assured me that I was the man for them. So, I found myself on my first day's filming, sitting very close to Lee Remick in a small buggy on a road in New England. She, a Bostonian by birth, was playing a European and speaking with an English accent. I was attempting to reply with a convincing American one, while trying to control the horse in full flight. It was autumn 1978 and the leaves on the trees were turning brilliant red and orange.

The colors were so extraordinary that when people saw the film in the UK, they thought we'd painted the trees!

Acton was a diffident character—and I didn't altogether enjoy playing him. I felt happier about getting to know rural America a little. The film took nearly three months to shoot and I enjoyed the experience.

Americans—and especially New Yorkers—are forthright and positive—not held back by excessive self-consciousness and irony. I found it a relief to park the defensive side of my Englishness for a while, shed a few layers of the onion and dive into the warm and convivial pool.

Poldark was shown on PBS—the *Public Broadcasting Service*—the nearest thing to the BBC that exists in America. PBS relies greatly on British drama exports and has provided British actors with a shop window they never enjoyed before.

Americans pay no TV license fee. As PBS is only partly funded by the government, it is chronically short of money. To persuade viewers to make donations, they organize pledge marathons—known by actors as "*begathons*".

Two Robins in Tintagel

For time to time I have been invited across to participate. I remember once accompanying a very reluctant Ian Carmichael on a walk round New York while he tried to persuade himself not to take the next plane back to England instead!

The evening involves mad shedding of further layers of the onion as the normally sedate and cautious guest celebrities turn into *"roll up, roll up"* Barnum and Bailey Ringmasters, cajoling and exhorting, teasing and persuading subscribers on the other end of the battery of phones to pledge their last nickel and dime.

Angharad and I also went to Madrid on a couple of promotional trips. It was 1980 and the series was already five years old to us, so it was a somewhat disembodied, detached *Ross* and *Demelza* who arrived at the airport to be greeted by 2,000 adoring Spanish fans eager to take us—literally—to their bosoms.

Poldark fever gripped Spain and for the moment we were the alternative King and Queen—and a right royal progress we made! We were naturally the subject of a great deal of speculation by the Spanish press.

Angharad was married with a family, so I became the focus of interest as a possible source of tasty scandal. I will never forget Angharad's exhortation as she saw me coming to the boil and about to explode: "Smile, Robin, for God's sake, smile!" Timely advice that I have heeded many times since!

Ross and *Demelza*

Spain featured strongly that year. Two promotion trips, a forgettable film and, oh dear—a TV commercial for men's underwear!

I had never done on-camera TV ads—not because I disapproved, but because I felt I wouldn't be any good at a straight sell without a character to hide behind. This Spanish commercial was a compromise. The ad-men wanted no mistaking who was hawking their brand of men's underpants. They insisted I be decked out as *Ross Poldark*. (*Well*, I thought, *at least I'll be dressed!*) The money was good so I did it! Shamelessly I stood in a studio in Wembley, spoke fluent Spanish (learned painfully by rote) and begged the young men of Spain to wear JIM underpants. I never found out whether the campaign was a success. Maybe it failed—nobody ever came back from holiday and confronted me with it!

One other experience stands out: It was a film for television made in the Valley of the Monkeys in Egypt.

I was home in London painting my bedroom when the telephone rang. It was Friday afternoon and the light outside was fading.

"Is your passport valid?" asked my agent.

"I don't know—let me look."

It was about to expire.

"Don't worry, they'll get you a new one. Are you free to go to Egypt on Sunday?" I looked at my half-painted bedroom and had no hesitation in saying yes.

With Harry Andrews outside Tutankhamun's tomb in Egypt

Ian McShane had broken his leg in a car accident during the shoot that afternoon. He had been playing *Howard Carter*, the discoverer of Tutankhamun's Burial Chamber in a TV movie memorably entitled *The Curse of King Tut's Tomb*. The producers decided to replace him immediately and by chance my dear friend

Angharad was in the film. She suggested me. I landed in Cairo on Sunday afternoon.

The Curse, it was said, was laid on anyone disturbing the Boy King's Tomb, and Lord Caernarvon—the son of Carter's patron— kept a very straight face when skeptical members of the cast treated the story with less than respect. Hadn't Ian McShane come to a sticky end after all? Joan Collins turned down a part in a blaze of publicity, saying she couldn't take the risk. Personally, I was blinded by gold and the chance to cross the Nile every day on my way to work. For me, the only curse was the script—which kept changing and whose authorship was less than clear.

We spent three weeks in Luxor—and another three in an aircraft hanger outside Bristol filming interiors. It gave me the opportunity to work with Harry Andrews—one of the finest actors of his generation; with Eva Marie Saint, who won an Oscar in her first film, *On The Waterfront,* with Marlon Brando; and with Raymond Burr, who had to remember all those questions as *Perry Mason* and *Ironside.* I survived the Curse and the script survived the ratings in America—beating out *Dallas* the night it aired.

Fair scene

Poldark perks peaked in the early eighties, but the goodwill has continued. One summer, for instance, at a friend's house, I met an American couple and their two-and-a-half year old daughter.

"You played *Poldark*, didn't you?" asked the husband. "You were *the first person* my daughter saw after being born. The TV was on in the labor ward."

I had to take his word for it as the daughter showed no signs of recognition.

In the past years, I haven't done as much acting as before. I have had a rest from it, earning my living from voice work—narrating documentaries and series like *End of Empire,* as well as voicing audio-visual presentations and TV and radio commercials. But maybe now is the time to get back to acting.

Robin Ellis' Album

My parents, Molly and Tony,
and two younger brothers, Peter and Jack—
a babe in arms, in my north London garden in 1955

Winston and Jean Graham at
our wedding reception in London (1990)

With my wife, Meredith Wheeler, at home in France (1995)

With Christopher Biggins (who played *Rev. Whitworth*) and brother, Jack, who was performing at the Theatre Royal Haymarket in Cambridge (2007)

Florence is one of my favorite cities in the world.
Tuscan cooking has always inspired me. (2011)

With my wife, Meredith, on the terrace at home in France (2005)

Signing copies of my cookbook, *Delicious Dishes for Diabetics*,
at Waterstone's bookstore in Truro, Cornwall (2011)

Autographing DVDs at Acorn Media in Silver Spring, Maryland
with then Senior Director Anne Kelleher. The complete *Poldark* series
in boxed set was released in 2012.

L'ail rose, pink garlic, air-drying in an open-sided barn at a
neighbor's farm. Lautrec holds a garlic festival
the first Friday of August every year. (2011)

Lautrec is a traditional *bastide* (fortified hilltop village),
and officially one of the *Most Beautiful Villages in France.*

With Meredith

Fooling around in silly hats
with Christopher Benjamin who played *Sir Hugh Bodrugan*

Serving lunch *al fresco* under the fig tree

Continuing the Saga

Twenty-five years on and I'm living in a presbytère (priest's house, though the last priest moved out about 70 years ago) deep in the countryside of southwestern France with an American wife, six cats and a hen!

I shop in the local open air markets and cook for the two of us twice a day. I've written a cookbook for type 2 diabetics, and I blog most days about that, cooking and life here.

What happened to the *actor* who for years feared the day when he discovered he didn't need to act anymore? What happened to the *townie* who found the countryside beautiful but *dull*—and couldn't wait to get back to the city on a Sunday night?

Well—"*life moves on*" is the easy answer, but that won't do.

When we reissued *Making Poldark* in the late '80s, Meredith and I were living in a Victorian house in north London, not far from where I grew up around Hampstead.

London is blessed with large parkland and Hampstead Heath was a brisk walk away; you can lose yourself in the woods there and make believe you are in the countryside while still being a short walk from the local movie house.

I had never thought of owning a second home in the sticks—let alone in France. I knew Italy better and went to Florence regularly. I love the Italian kitchen.

However I found myself in the *départment* of the Tarn with Meredith to visit one of her old pals from ABC News, the Texan correspondent and anchorman, Hughes Rudd. A great Francophile, he and his wife Ann had built their retirement home not far from Albi.

It was a shock to hear myself asking Hughes and his friends if they knew of anyone selling a house. They did. More shocking still, after a quick look, I found myself offering the owner the asking price five hours later! Not exactly driving a hard bargain—but I'd fallen in love (*coup de foudre*) again! It was 1990.

Meredith (*coup de foudre Number 1* back in 1986) and I were getting married that summer and she must have been asking herself: *Do I need this with the wedding coming too?*

We were married in August at the Rosslyn Hill Unitarian Chapel in Hampstead (north London) and had our reception at the London Zoo. That zoo has a famous association with pandas and one of our guests, Jim Carter (now famous for playing the butler in *Downton Abbey*), was persuaded to don a panda bear costume and cut in on Meredith and me as we danced the traditional bride and groom's first dance!

We honeymooned at the French house—empty apart from a large wooden bed made by a friend that we had to assemble in order to sleep on it. Our first purchase was a mattress.

I thought: I've bought a house 700 miles from London! It's a foreign land, we barely speak French and the only local people we know are Hughes and Ann—who live an hour's drive north.

Nevertheless we resolved to go there often—to make it an extension of our lives in London rather than simply a holiday home. I decided to set aside a yearly sum for the monthly visits to the house.

In addition to these we planned to spend longer periods there at Christmas, Easter and in the summer—when we would drive down.

We signed up for a weekly dose of French at *l'Institut Français* in South Kensington—four hours on Wednesday mornings with an interesting group of fellow sufferers, some of whom are still friends.

Clearly we were serious.

Nina de Voogd Fuller—the Dutch-American owner of the house—helped with practical details like setting up bank accounts and passing on her builder, carpenter and plumber. We had bought blind—no idea even where the nearest town was—so Nina's help was golden.

Neighbors called by to say *bonjour*—curious to inspect these *étrangers*.

The house sits between a church and small cemetery. The year 1715 is carved into the stone lintel above the front door. On the winter solstice in cold December, the sun sets directly opposite; in a summer heat wave thick walls keep the house as cool as the best air-conditioning. Those Ancients knew a thing or two!

Gradually we began to put down roots. The neighbor who is an accountant helped us fill out French documents and told stories of walking across the fields barefoot as a boy to attend catechism with the local priest in what is now our kitchen.

Our carpenter who was born in the nearest *hameau* did the same. He invited us to his home in Castres to show us how to preserve *foie gras* in the traditional southwest way.

The farmers who own most of the land around us gave us old roof tiles to repair the *pigeonnier* and a colony of bees so we could try our hand with a hive.

Every stray cat in the area heard about *les Anglais* and Meredith found herself running a cat sanctuary. One pregnant queen came by on the 11th of June so we called her *Onze*. She had three kittens in our laundry basket.

Her owners spotted her by the road one day and turned up to claim her. Thus began our friendship with Florence and Thierry, our neighbors and oldest *amis* in *le coin*.

A decade and more into a new century and here we are still—with *six* cats and a hen!

The Series That Never Was

The original two series of *Poldark* are being viewed now by a third generation—thanks to videocassette and DVDs—40 years after we first went to Cornwall in Spring of 1975.

Its endurance says much for the storytelling skills of Winston Graham, who wrote the original four books in the immediate post-war years. Happily for me and my fellow actors the many attempts to film the story came to nothing until the BBC went ahead in the mid-seventies.

We filmed seven of the books in the series and Winston went on to write five more—publishing the twelfth and last of the sequence, *Bella Poldark* in 2002, a year before he died aged 95.

There was an attempt to film a third series in the mid-nineties which was unsuccessful.

In January 1995 the commercial British television company, HTV, approached Angharad Rees and me with a proposal to make a two-hour pilot of the eighth *Poldark* book, *The Stranger from the Sea*.

The expectation was that this would air as a Christmas Special later that year and we would go on to make a third series if it proved popular.

Winston had written four more *Poldark* novels in the intervening years.

The Angry Tide, the last book in the second TV series, finished in 1799—so the characters had all moved on a decade. The notion of playing the same characters 10 years older intrigued us both.

The central thrust of the narrative in these new novels was taken up by the next generation of the *Poldark* and *Warleggan* families. *Ross* and *Demelza* naturally found their place as the older generation of the new story lines Winston developed.

It felt right, organic, a truthful progression—something we could believe in and play with conviction.

We had friendly meetings with the producers and our agents talked terms. We agreed to hold ourselves available to film in May and June, preceded by a period for rehearsal.

A script was commissioned.

I noted in my diary Angharad's enthusiastic summing up: *"Here we go then, my darling!"*

Well—no, we didn't in the end!

Delay followed delay with the script. When it was finally finished it was rejected.

The problem was simple: How to fit a 400 page book into a two-hour movie. We were, after all, doing more than a one-off movie; the pilot was in principle setting up a series.

It gradually became clear that HTV only wanted Angharad and me from the original cast. They did not intend to use the original music and were distancing themselves from the original as much as they dared.

In early April, after a script conference with the production team we came away feeling that progress had made. We'd been heard sympathetically.

They commissioned a new script from a different writer and we were hopeful.

After a month, I received a letter from the producer. Reading between the lines, it was obvious that whatever we had hoped for, whatever we felt might be right for the project, the changes we had agreed upon were now in doubt. Her hands were tied. She would do her best, but she was obliged to fulfill the brief given to her by the all-powerful ITV Drama Network Centre.

The days when creative producers could come up with an idea and guide it through to the screen, without interference from a controlling authority, were plainly over.

However much we howled—and there was some howling—she was powerless.

The new script was delayed and filming was put back to September. We were now in July and our enthusiasm was waning.

Meredith and I went to a friend's wedding in Chicago—out of the frying pan and into the fire as it turned out.

We flew into the hottest mid-July the Windy City had experienced since 1934—106°F on the day of the festivities. Hundreds of Chicagoans died from the heat. The wedding was black tie—so I was in a tuxedo and Meredith in a long black dress—trying to stay cool.

Nevertheless, it was a welcome diversion from the tension building back home.

I remember eating corn on the cob—picked that day—in neighboring Wisconsin (where we'd gone to escape the urban heat wave).

Blissful—one of the simplest and most delicious eats you can have—but (according to my Midwestern in-laws) they have to be eaten the same day they are picked!

Back in the UK it all went wrong.

The formal negotiations over our fees became a confused nightmare. The fee offer from HTV was drastically reduced—by half! Our agents had agreed to our salary back in February—but no documents had been signed. The gentleman's agreement was apparently being jettisoned.

Back and forth it went with very little coming 'forth' from the company. They were not giving an inch on anything—and I felt bad about it.

One weekday in August, Meredith and I went on a canoe trip on the river Aveyron, an hour to the north of us, for a bit of peace and quiet.

I had no idea a final deadline had been set by the company. We had until the end of business *that* day, to accept their offer.

The Executive Producer waited all afternoon by the phone, we were told later—but no one rang.

He telephoned the next morning and said the deal was off—they were looking elsewhere.

My agent told me it was my last chance—I was 53 and I should plead for a change of heart. I did—reluctantly. I wrote letters and my agent tried to negotiate—to no avail.

They were adamant. There was no going back. This *Ross* and *Demelza* had finally hung up their boots and bonnets!

The pilot was filmed in the autumn but did *not* air at Christmas, as originally planned.

Reports filtered out and they were not encouraging for HTV. *The Independent* newspaper reported in September 1995:

> *Winston Graham's Poldark, presently being dramatized by HTV, is a saga of love and hatred, loyalty and betrayal, tragedy and passion. Unfortunately the film itself has aroused exactly the same emotions.*

Still they insisted its non-appearance at Christmas was nothing to do with doubts about the production's advertising pulling power—but just a wish to show it later the following year.

Of course it was disappointing not to have done it. It would have been fascinating to have played *Ross* again 10–15 years older—but it was not to be.

Fame and fortune? *"Your last chance, Robin..."* Well yes—perhaps I shouldn't have been so complacent about that doubtful double act. But in truth I wasn't as driven as an actor as I had been in the '70s.

I remember dear Ralph Bates—so memorable as *George Warleggan*—coming up to me as I paced the corridor outside the studio in Birmingham, waiting to record an episode of the second series. He patted me kindly on the shoulder and whispered in my ear, *"You know it's only a play, Robin!"*

We were five years into the ownership of this 18th century rectory in southwestern France. We were getting to know and like the region. I loved shopping in the local markets, and surprised myself at how increasingly drawn I felt to a life in the country.

Before moving on from the *"Sad Case of a Third Series Unachieved"*, I must mention the Poldark Appreciation Society, which played an astounding role—in fact, the only fully *costumed* role—in the whole frustrating saga.

Founded by enthusiast Val Adams from Cornwall, they were an extraordinary and fiercely loyal group of *Poldark* fans and aficionados.

Angharad, Winston and I and other *Poldark* alumni would regularly attend their annual lunch gatherings in London and got to know many of them and appreciate their devotion to the series.

HTV had not reckoned on their passionate commitment to the original cast or their ability to generate a juicy story. They picketed HTV's offices both in Bristol and their London base on Bond Street in full 18th century costume. The media loved it. The show's Executive Producer was forced to meet with Val and afterwards she told *The Independent*'s journalist, that

"It wouldn't have mattered if they'd cast Richard Burton and Elizabeth Taylor. The point is that no one else can play *Ross* and *Demelza.*"

Ultimately they failed to persuade HTV to change its mind about the casting, but they generated a good deal of unwelcome publicity for the company, which must have been ruing the day it had ever embarked on the project.

John Bowe was cast as *Ross* and Mel Martin as *Demelza*. They are both fine actors but the pilot was not well received and no further episodes in the series were commissioned.

The BBC version was 29 hours of canter and trot—this was television—spinning out the tales of seven books. Each book had about four hours of screen time.

HTV planned to gallop through five books in 10 hours—and fell at the first hurdle.

They lost out on more than a horse race.

The video sales for the two series were impressive. Only *Pride and Prejudice* had sold more at that time.

Sylvia

I n the Chinese calendar, 1996 was the Year of the Rat. For me, it was the year of the Dog!

Early in March I was sent a copy of a play called *Sylvia* by the American playwright, P. J. (Pete) Gurney. Unusually, it was set to go straight into the *West End*—no pre-London tour.

I hadn't been on stage for 20 years, so I was surprised. Zoe Wanamaker, a friend, was starring as the eponymous *Sylvia*—a stray dog found in Manhattan's Central Park.

I went to see the veteran theatre director Michael Blakemore with whom I'd worked in the late sixties. He was directing and—no messing about—I was offered the part.

The play is set in New York City, and is a nicely surreal comedy about a married couple's mid-life crisis.

It opens as *Greg* (my character) brings *Sylvia* back to his West Side apartment.

Zoe—with a platinum blonde rinse—was playing a dog! Maria Aitken was playing my wife, *Kate*.

In 1976, I'd spent an engrossing year at Stratford-on-Avon with the *Royal Shakespeare Company*—but hadn't *trod the boards* since. I was a little nervous!

We rehearsed at the *Old Vic*, in the large rehearsal room at the top of this iconic building. Ghosts—again—were in the walls, watching. Laurence Olivier had rehearsed for his *Othello* in this space and Maggie Smith and Robert Stevens had sharpened their *Beatrice* and *Benedick* here.

The rehearsals went well—though I was rusty. *Greg* was the longest role I'd played on stage where—unlike television or film—you have to remember *all* the lines *all* the time!

I'd ride my bicycle back home to Chalk Farm from Waterloo after rehearsals, eat a quick supper and disappear to the top of the house to cram in the lines. I'd stagger down a couple of hours later to ask a tolerant Meredith whether she'd mind for the umpteenth time running me through them.

There was also the small matter of the American accent.

Zoe was born of American parents—father Sam came to the UK to escape the McCarthy witch-hunts in the fifties—so the accent was in her. I had played Americans on film but sustaining an accent without recourse to re-takes was a new challenge.

On the other hand, an accent can help you. Speaking with an American accent changes my body language; I become loose-limbed, more expansive, more expressive.

Greg was not a loud mouth and perhaps that's what attracted *Sylvia*—who barked above her weight. She tolerated his occasional drifts into philosophical musings while the two of them gazed at the stars on evening walks in the Park, saying simply: "*I wish I could contribute something here, but I just plain can't.*" She really only wanted to be near him!

We managed a short weekend in France before the play opened and I remember having distinctly ambivalent feelings about the possibility of not being free to return for a stretch, if the play was a success.

I had done two six-month runs in West End theatre and found both stultifying. Doing the same play night after night is a special kind of torture!

I enjoyed the rehearsals for *Sylvia*—difficult though they were at times. One Wednesday I was thoroughly ticked off by Michael for not knowing the lines. I wanted to shout at him: *"I'm trying for %#*&~@'s sake!"*

I was *trying*—but perhaps not quite *match-fit*.

Zoe—whom I'd known for years but never worked with—*was* match-fit. It was her first eponymous starring role in the West End and she was very focused. Every spare minute we would run the lines—fortunately for me.

Maria Aitkin, I had never met before. She was happily combining a successful acting career with directing theatre in New York, where she lived.

The fourth member of the cast—tasked with playing three parts—one in drag—was the very experienced Neil McCaul.

We were a happy quartet, working hard with a starry director—Michael, and a supportive and ebullient producer, Michael Redington.

Sylvia was an unusual comedy by an established and successful playwright. You can never legislate for success in the theatre, but the signs augured well.

We opened at the *Apollo Theatre* on Shaftesbury Avenue (London's equivalent of Broadway) on April 20. My name was up in lights for the first and only time!

Meredith was at least as nervous as me on the first night. She had decorated my poky dressing room to make it as comfortable as possible. Knowing how much I was missing France, she even hung a framed poster of Cezanne's painting of a French hillside village, reminiscent of Lautrec.

However many previews you have done, First Nights are always an ordeal—even though the audience is usually willing you to succeed.

It seemed to go well.

There was an enthusiastic welcome at the party afterwards. I remember feeling buoyant and relieved at dinner. Zoe, dining with her mother at another table, was the same.

However the reviews that followed over the next few days were decidedly mixed.

Zoe's performance was universally praised and the rest of us escaped largely unhurt. It was the play that the critics went for, accusing it of sentimentality and silliness.

Michael Redington wrote us a note of encouragement that included the news that Stoll Moss, the theatre owners, "were very pleased with the show and expressed their determination to do all they can to make *Sylvia* a success."

Reminiscent of what happens soon after a Prime Minister or Chief Executive expresses total confidence in a troubled Minister or employee—they sack them!

Two weeks after opening night we were told we'd be closing in a week!

The audiences were small but enthusiastic. It was clearly a *feel good* piece that didn't appeal to critics and needed time for word of mouth to spread. With new shows always knocking at the gates, this was too long to wait.

They say there are advantages to being in a flop. You get the notices but don't have to spend the next six months repeating it night after night!

Zoe got the notices and went from strength to strength.

I enjoyed the experience—and if I'm honest was relieved not to have to continue for a long run. I could now look forward to a summer in France.

There's a happy epilogue to the *Sylvia* saga.

Zoe's husband, Gawn Grainger, had not seen the production because he was in a play himself, which closed the same night as we did.

To give Gawn a chance to see Zoe, on Wednesday evening of the following week we performed the whole play in Maria Aitken's large garden in Kennington to a select audience—with Gawn as guest of honor. He presided sitting on a throne-like chair in the middle of the group.

The garden setting doubled well for Central Park. It might have been the best performance we gave. Certainly Maria's cat enjoyed it.

It wandered in and out and under our feet until Zoe turned at an opportune moment and growled at it—in character! It never came back!

Voice-Overs

After *Sylvia*, life resumed its more familiar rhythms—the weekly routine of voice-overs and commentaries with the now keenly anticipated weekend visits to France.

My voice-over career had started back in the early 1980s when Jenni Waters—a specialist agent—wrote to ask if I had ever thought of doing voice work. I hadn't and she took me on.

I recorded a show tape to demonstrate my range. She would send this *demo tape* to potential bookers at the advertising agencies.

I am what the business calls a *brown voice*—a warm and reassuring sell.

Five years later, I took this tape to New York to play to Meredith, whom I was courting. Far from being impressed with my expertise and charmed by the *voice beautiful*, she *hated* it!

"You don't sound anything like the real you—so unctuous and oozing with 'sell!' Ick!"

My first taste of Meredith's uncompromising critical honesty! It's a quality I've come to appreciate and trust—though sometimes through gritted teeth (knowing in my heart that she's usually right).

Jenni was getting bookings for me. It was only four years since the second series of *Poldark* had aired and some producers were curious to get a close-up look at me.

They would book me for a test—with a fee attached. If the client liked the result we would re-do it (another fee) or they would use the original. Either way repeats were payable.

I began to understand why actors' views about doing commercials—often snooty—were changing. It could be very profitable in lean times and help support the mainline acting career, allowing them to refuse jobs that weren't quite right.

My own "mainline" career was flattening out. I'd turned forty in 1982 and my days as a young leading man were numbered.

I found the day-to-day immediacy of this new voice-over world enjoyable and challenging.

Jenni might call me at the flat in Chelsea in the morning to say: You have a booking at John Wood's studio in Soho—12pm to 1pm for the *TV Times*. It's a test, but likely to go if all goes well.

The producer would hand me the script as I settled into the cramped soundproof booth with a view of the big screen through the glass. Big John Wood would take a voice level and then run the thirty-second commercial.

I'd stumble through a first reading with one eye on the screen, trying to hit the key points in the script. It might take three or four attempts before I'd find the right rhythm that matched the images on screen.

The creative team—who were hearing a professional voice speak the words with the pictures for the first time—would complicate the task by changing the script or suggesting line readings.

Panic is the enemy, as the brain struggles to stay calm and assimilate these demands. The experience and skill of the engineer plays a big part and John Wood helped me through some difficult sessions in those early days.

By the mid-'80s, I was on more solid ground. I learned to hang my ego on the hat stand outside the studio before going into the booth! I was there to do the bidding of the creative team; they had chosen my *voice* (not me as an *actor*) as the sound best suited to sell their product.

It had taken four years of being available at an hour's notice to get known and trusted by the major agencies—as a *voice*.

Jenni was a skilled negotiator and the concentrated effort began to pay off—we were a good team. We decided to set up a voice-over agency. Jenni would run it and the bank accepted me as the financial guarantor.

We soon built a client list from the increasing number of actors wanting to "get into voice-overs" for that extra income.

Voices started life in a tiny office two flights up in Wardour Street, Soho—walking distance from most of the sound studios where the sessions were held.

I cycled from home to work all over London riding my 1938 Raleigh stand-up-and-beg no gears bicycle with a basket on the front. It was the surest way to get to a session *on time* in an often gridlocked city, where public transport was ever more unreliable.

I enjoyed the independence it gave me (and the occasional naughtiness of taking a short cut the wrong way up a one-way street!). According to my odometer I notched up over 10,000 miles nipping in and out of Central London over nearly 20 years. The work was paying for frequent trips to France and repairs on the old *presbytère*.

Important this, because as the epic year of 2000 approached, Meredith and I thought a gesture to the new Millennium was in order.

After 10 years of working as a psychotherapist in London, she was ready for a change too. We don't have children and our parents were no longer alive. Without ties binding us to London, we decided to try a permanent move to France.

Moving to France

On the Fourth of July, 1999—Independence Day in America—we gave ourselves a *bon voyage* party at the Organic Café in Kilburn. (Eating well—and healthily—was a preoccupation even back then!)

Decked out in red, white and blue with all things American—Meredith's handiwork, of course—the restaurant was a pretty sight.

Friends came from far and wide to drink to our new life. After a sit-down dinner and speeches, we cleared a space and danced. Meredith had hired a jukebox for the evening and had it stocked with our favorite old rock 'n roll hits.

No nickels or dimes were required! Guests just pressed the buttons for golden oldies, and old 45s would be selected by the automatic arm and lifted onto the turntable. It was a celebration as well as a *farewell* to England.

Many—including ourselves perhaps—had a hard time believing we were really leaving. It was disturbing to some. We were asked a lot of questions that boiled down to: *Why? What are you going to do there?* and *Have you ever spent a winter there?*

Of course everyone wished us well—though perhaps some wondered how long it would be before we'd be back!

Others at the party had already stayed with us in the French house and understood what attracted us to the way of life there. They realized that it was not just a holiday home.

In nine years we had put down some roots, made friends, even acquired cats—who uncannily would be waiting for us when we arrived. (Our dear French friends, Thierry and Flo, kept them when we weren't there—but the cats seemed to sense when we were coming—despite the irregular intervals. Flo said they would just suddenly disappear, walking the quarter mile to our house.)

But for those who had yet to visit us *there*, our departure was puzzling—and even a little hurtful.

We weren't leaving because we hated London—we were going because we wanted to try living in southwestern France—a life in a charming old house in stunning countryside, good climate and wonderful open air markets.

Simple as that.

I remember standing in the street outside our London house in Chalk Farm, waving farewell to Michael King's small removal van— full of our furniture and paintings. What happened then and how we arrived definitively days later in France is a blank!

It's a fair bet though that soon after arrival, we sat in the kitchen and pondered the preceding 13 years—and all the forces that brought us here.

Flashback!

Flashback to January 1986: Just turned 44, I was one of a dozen or so British actors invited to America by WGBH (the public TV station in Boston) to celebrate the 15th anniversary of *Masterpiece Theater*, the PBS program, hosted then by Alistair Cooke, that introduced the American public to many British TV series—mainly costume dramas—from the original *Forsythe Saga* to Jane Austen to Paul Scott's *Raj Quartet*. Indeed it was the season of *Jewel in the Crown* and many of the leading actors were part of our group: Tim Piggott-Smith, Susan Wooldridge and Ian Richardson.

Also on the trip were Diana Rigg, Susan Hampshire, Nicol Williamson and Simon Williams. *Poldark* has been popular with the American public, so I was invited too.

Now renamed simply *Masterpiece*, the program celebrated its fortieth anniversary in 2010—making it the longest running prime time drama on American television. It remains an excellent showcase for British actors and frequently co-produces many Anglo-American productions screened on both sides of the Atlantic—like *Downton Abbey*, the current hit.

Back in 1986 the show was sponsored by Mobil Oil, which flew us on the supersonic Concorde from London to Boston (just three-

and-a-half hours!) where we were wined, dined, interviewed and celebrated.

Then from a snow-bound Boston we took a four-hour train ride to New York City for a gala night at the St Regis Hotel where—though I didn't know it—my fate would be sealed.

Meredith had been hired by a magazine program at NBC News to do a story on the anniversary celebrations of *Masterpiece Theater*. That included interviewing the British actors and filming the elaborate reception hosted by New York Mayor Ed Koch at the elegant midtown hotel.

Meredith was a *Poldark* fan and was rather disappointed when she interviewed me that I didn't have a ponytail and a face scar!

She is a born listener and it had stood her in good stead as a journalist and would do so again in her future calling as a psychotherapist. I found her easy to talk to, even though I was on camera.

At one point, though, I *dried* (theatre speak for *became lost for words*) as I stared into her deep brown eyes. She repeated the question and I managed to finish the interview.

That evening at the gala reception with hundreds of New Yorkers in Black Tie finery, Meredith winked at me from her position behind the camera on the other side of the ballroom.

She always claims that fateful wink was simply a *thumbs-up* sign to me—*you're alright there*—as I chatted to a couple of attractive young women.

I didn't see it that way and detaching myself—politely I hope—walked over to the camera position.

A waiter coming towards me with a tray full of brimming champagne flutes, anxious to avoid a collision, didn't notice the camera cord on the floor and tripped, emptying *bubbly* all over my tuxedo.

Meredith kindly says I was very *Cary Grant* about it; I think I was so distracted by the *wink*, I barely noticed my soaking shirtfront!

At the end of the reception this motley bunch of British actors had nowhere to go to let off steam. Meredith, seizing the moment as only she can, rang *Limelight*, the nightclub of the moment in a converted church in lower Manhattan.

"I am a producer with NBC and am hosting a party of British actors. They are only in New York briefly and they want to come by tonight."

Set up in a deconsecrated church on Sixth Avenue at 20th Street, it was notoriously difficult to gain entry. But her *chutzpah* paid off—and we were ushered straight into the VIP lounge on arrival.

Tired and jetlagged we were, yet we danced and talked our heads off.

Meredith and I waltzed the place to a close at 3am, then with Tim Pigott-Smith, we headed for the famous *10th Avenue Diner*—where we drank vodka until 4am.

The actors flew home—Concorde again—two days later and the following night I went out to dinner with my brother, Jack.

"I've met the woman I'm going to marry!" I told him.

This was questionable *chutzpah* on my part—as she was already married to someone else!

And so it started.

I returned to New York 13 times that year and Meredith did the reverse journey five times. Then in 1987 she left her marriage and the States to be with me in London. We found a house in Camden and settled down. In 1990 we were married at Rosslyn Hill Unitarian Chapel in Hampstead.

The role of *Colonel Mustard* in a television series of *Cluedo*—not the high point of my acting career—paid for the reception at the London Zoo!

It was a momentous year—we also bought the house in France and Meredith began studies to become a psychotherapist. I continued to do voiceovers and the occasional acting work.

Back to the Kitchen
and Into the Next Century!

France is one of the few European countries where *Poldark* was never shown. Being recognized is a rare occurrence anywhere these days. In France I only remember it happening once.

On a freezing December afternoon, not long after our move, I was shopping in Castres, our local town. The pavement was icy and treacherous outside *Monoprix*. I was about to enter when a middle-aged woman slipped and fell in front of me. As I bent down to help her, she looked up at me and after a startled pause said:

"*What are YOU doing HERE?*" in heavily accented English. Taken aback, I said, "*I live here now!*"

"*I know you—you are Poldark,*' she exclaimed—so loudly that my first instinct was to deny it!

"Well, yes—uh—I PLAYED *Poldark* a long time ago in England...."

She was now on her feet and we were face to face.

"I saw you on TV in Canada—Vancouver—where I live."

She recovered quickly from the two consecutive shocks and explained that she was in France visiting her sister for Christmas. She had enjoyed watching *Poldark* in Canada in the late '70s.

Having completed this initial rather surreal conversation in the freezing cold, I agreed to meet her and her sister for a coffee after the holidays.

This chance encounter had a strange twist. When Meredith and I met Yvette, the mystery lady from Canada, it turned out that her sister was the estate agent who had once been charged with the sale of our house on behalf of the previous owner.

From her we learned that shortly before we stumbled on the house, an American man—after much hemming and hawing—had decided to buy it.

After a final viewing of the property, he left by car for Castres to sign the papers initiating the sale. Madame Barthes was waiting for him at her agency. When he failed to turn up, she telephoned the owner of the house who confirmed that the prospective buyer had set off long before. A search was launched.

It turned out the unfortunate American had a serious automobile accident on his way to Castres at a dangerous turning on the road. He spent the next six months in hospital and, so we were told, limps to this day! The sale was abandoned.

Soon afterwards, we walked into the courtyard under a double rainbow and I fell in love (again)!

So in some way, we suspect the house *found us!*

Winston Graham

Winston Graham died on July 10, 2003. He was 95 and had completed the twelfth and final *Poldark* novel, *Bella Poldark*, the previous year—rounding off the remarkable saga that he first launched in 1945 with *Ross Poldark*.

I remember being gripped by the powerful narrative drive and the sheer scope and fun of his last book. He had fallen in love with his leading lady—again—and was fully committed to doing her justice. It was a remarkable *tour de force* at that late stage in his life.

I was reminded of why the whole saga had been such a long-lived popular success. Put simply, he wrote good stories with believable characters whose lives—though lived in a different era—we cared about.

Winston finished his autobiography, *Memoirs of a Private Man*, shortly before his death and Angharad and I accompanied his son Andrew and daughter Rosamund to Truro in Cornwall for the official launch.

He had been born in Manchester and lived there until he was 17. When his father died at 53 in the aftermath of a stroke, the family moved to Perranporth in Cornwall in 1925.

There he married Jean Williamson, a Cornish girl, whom he'd first met when she was 13 (the same age as *Demelza* when she first met *Ross*) and he was 18 (younger than *Ross* when he first met *Demelza*).

There they lived for the next 25 years and there they brought up Andrew and Rosamund.

Graham was always meticulous and thorough in his research. By the time he wrote *Ross Poldark*, he knew much about the history and customs of Cornwall and the Cornish.

The authenticity of place and character shines through the books—the reader feels in good hands.

For the actors it was invaluable being able to refer to a well-crafted narrative with highly developed characters whose behavior had been thought through. This landed me in trouble, as I mentioned earlier, with the notorious scene 13A in Episode Seven [see page 35] when I referred back to the original text.

It wasn't simply that I was right and the adaptor was wrong; *Winston* was right—and the adaptor had ignored him. Having played Winston's *Poldark* for six hour-long episodes, I felt the tug of the original writer's imagination.

Winston touched on this in his book *Poldark's Cornwall*. In giving his reasons for turning down the opportunity to do a third BBC *Poldark* series in 1978 based on *storylines* (not books), he writes:

> *"However one judges the books, they are organic, character leading to action, action leading to a further development of character. To have written thirteen episodes, even with a sympathetic script-writer, would have introduced a new element of haste and contrivance into the series. Apart from the public, it would somehow have been letting down the fictional people about whom I have come to care so much."*

Thank you, Winston—I rest my case!

I will always feel appreciative of Winston for writing such a wonderful tale that meant so much in my own life. And I was touched when Winston inscribed a copy of *Ross Poldark* to me with these words:

Dear Robin,

I have so far watched twelve installments with hypercritical gaze and have never seen you put a foot wrong. You've played many parts and will have many more, but I doubt if you'll play another character in which you achieve a greater identity with what the author intended, or give him—and about ten million other people—so much pleasure.

Winston
Christmas 1975

Winston Graham's Album

Winston Graham, in a cameo role, played a Cornish gent.

Michael Cadman played *Dr. Dwight Enys*
in the second series, replacing Richard Morant.

Brian Stimer played *Hugh Armitage*, *Demelza*'s other love interest and
Ross' rival. A crowd of fans on the hill watch the filming.

Julie Dawn Cole played *Rowella Chynoweth*.

Elizabeth and *George Warleggan*
played by Jill Townsend and Ralph Bates.

Jane Wymark (*Morwenna*) and Kevin McNally (*Drake*)

Stefan Gates played *Geoffrey Charles Poldark*
and grew up to write cookbooks, too.

Trudie Styler appeared in three episodes
of the second series playing *Emma Tregirls*.

Footmen extras taking the weight off their feet!

Jill Townsend as *Elizabeth* steps out of period for a puff!

Winston and Jean Graham offering
George Warleggan (Ralph Bates) some support

Jean Graham and the odious *Rev. Whitworth*
(the genial Christopher Biggins)

Winston Graham with the lovely *Morwenna* (Jane Wymark)

Kevin McNally (*Drake Carne*) uses his break to entertain.

Drake and *Sam Carne* (Kevin McNally and David Delve)

Kitchen Matters

There's no reference in the books to *Ross Poldark* being active in the kitchen of Nampara (the house he'd inherited from his father).

My guess is he wouldn't have known how to boil an egg or even where the saucepans were kept!

Prudie might have taught him to fry a few freshly caught pilchards, when she couldn't be bothered to make *starry gazey* pie. She was a better cook than housekeeper as I remember.

I'd have been eager to learn—if I'd been *him!*

Unlike *Ross*, I learned to cook at my mother's knee. That's about where I came up to the first time I remember being allowed to lick out the cake bowl. What ambrosia it seemed, that delicious, buttery mix—crunchy with undissolved sugar—that clung to the sides of the big, brown bowl.

My mother made all manner of cakes. Fruit cake with icing for festivals like Christmas, sponges for Sundays and scones for special teatimes.

One such tea ended with a ticking off for me—or should have.

Auntie Rita—no relative, I'm sure—was due at 4pm for tea and scones (how times have changed!). Ma was flustered and as the hour approached she sighed to herself, loud enough for *big ears* to overhear: *Oh, Rita's the last thing I need....*

The front bell rang and I ran to open the door. There was Rita. *"Mummy doesn't want you to come to tea today, Auntie Rita!"*

I don't think we ever saw Rita again.

"Helping" my mother in the kitchen was part of growing up. Licking out the bowl, smelling the Seville oranges boiling and bubbling on the cooker in February for marmalade, watching the slow drip of milk through muslin making cottage cheese or groaning as Ma added rennet and sugar to boiled milk to make junket—a disgusting, limp dessert that I dreaded!

It was *sous-cheffing* of a low order, but it left me with an understanding that to eat well—which we did, thanks to a talented and interested mother—*effort* is required.

There was a room we called the Dining Room in my childhood home in Hampstead Garden Suburb in the fifties. It was rarely used—at Christmas, perhaps, when Dad would build a fire in there.

Our house had no central heating—so every reason to stay in the parlour-like kitchen where the stove kept us warm. We ate all our meals at a well-scrubbed rectangular pine table. In a way I've been eating at that table and cooking in that kitchen ever since.

The Cookbook

W
hy don't you write a cookbook, Robin?

A cookbook? That's a bit of a leap! I like to cook—in fact that's mainly what I do now—twice a day—lunch and dinner. I do almost all the marketing too, mainly at open-air markets in the towns and villages around us.

But a cookbook...? Weren't there too many cooks writing too many cookbooks? And I wasn't a professional. It was flattering that family and friends suggested it, but I was reluctant.

My resistance stayed firm for some time—for a few years in fact! I was happy cooking for Meredith and visiting family and friends.

I continued collecting recipes, pasting them in a red foolscap notebook—Ma had done the same in a blue one. We clearly shared an urge to search out reliable recipes.

Brother Jack and sister-in-law Christine kept my bookshelves up-to-date with the newest cookbooks—as did friends who knew I'd be delighted with any new addition.

The pressure was growing though!

When Meredith noticed me writing up a few recipes for the fun of it, she began to say at lunch and dinner tables, *"Robin is working on a cookbook!"*

"Really—what a good idea!"

"Um—yes. I'm enjoying it—we'll see...."

Then on subsequent visits the first question to me was: *"How's the cookbook going, Robin?"*

"Um—fine, thanks—slowly."

Around this time I'd started working with a laptop—more practical than the desktop computer in my office.

One afternoon I found myself sitting in the shade under the trees in the garden, experimenting with an introduction to the putative book!

Clearly I had started believing in the idea myself.

The following summer, Timberlake Wertenbaker—author of the wonderful play, *Our Country's Good* (amongst many others!), emailed me from her home in the Basque country asking for recipe ideas for entertaining. She liked to cook but was too busy working to search for new dishes.

It was a tipping point.

I realized that I had accumulated a range of interesting recipes ready to send off. These later formed the basis of the collection that Meredith packaged up to test the publishing waters for a book.

The initial responses were courteous but unproductive. Unless you are a TV chef/cook, restaurateur or have a current celebrity profile, it is hard to interest the cash-strapped publishing establishment—their way of doing business already under threat from eBooks and the internet.

One friend—an established cookery writer, four books under her belt—had the greatest difficulty getting her most recent work on French cooking published. Eventually she found a publisher—but it's tough out there!

Meredith then had a brainwave. It was obvious in a way, but one doesn't always see clearly what is staring you in the face. The book could be angled towards people with the same condition as me: those with type 2 diabetes.

Diabetes

Soon after moving to France permanently, I was diagnosed with type 2 diabetes (sometimes called *late-onset* or *adult onset* diabetes).

It was picked up in a routine PSA blood test to check for prostate cancer (undertaken at the urging of an old school friend who had been diagnosed with that illness).

The prostate was fine, but the test showed elevated levels of glucose (sugar) in my blood. My French doctor spotted the danger and ran another test a few months later that confirmed the diagnosis.

It was a disease well known to me. My mother had died from a heart attack, related to her 30-year battle with type 1 diabetes (the kind that requires daily injections of insulin).

I had seen, first hand, how destructive it could be—what a toll it can take on someone's body over time. The suddenness of her demise had shocked me.

One morning in early December 1982 she was dressing to go shopping after breakfast. My father heard a noise from their bedroom and went up to investigate. He found her lying dead on the carpet. She had had a massive heart attack—a not-infrequent side effect of diabetes.

Having experienced the trauma of Ma's death and knowing the difficulties and complications she'd endured beforehand, I quickly took on board the potential dangers of this insidious condition.

I was lucky. There are few pronounced symptoms in the early stages of type 2 diabetes, so some people find it difficult to take it seriously—and are reluctant to make changes to their daily routine. That was not the case for me.

After a week or so of *why me?* and *c'est pas vrai!* behavior, I faced facts, bought some books and started to read up about it.

A friend put me onto Michel Montignac's book *Dine Out and Lose Weight* in which the author talks of adopting *a way of eating* rather than *dieting* as a means of losing weight and keeping it off—a crucial element in the control of type 2 diabetes.

Montignac grew up in southwestern France—where eating well and *plentifully* is a way of life—and had inherited his family's tendency to obesity. He believed that *diets* were only a short-term fix—and rarely effective in the long run. He researched another approach, which he described like this:

"There is no deprivation and it is not a diet. It is more a lifestyle. It is designed not only to aid weight loss in the short term, but also to help people maintain their weight loss long term by advocating healthy eating habits, which can also prevent illness and disease."

Montignac was an early advocate of the *glycemic index*—which measures the effect of carbohydrates on blood sugar levels (how quickly carbohydrates turn to glucose in the blood)—to help people lose weight.

He distinguished good carbs (unrefined with a low glycemic index) from bad (a high glycemic index) and asserted that it is the high sugar content in bad carbs that encourage the body to store unwanted fat. He did not believe that high calorie intake *per se* added weight.

I made adjustments in what I ate. Out went white rice, white bread and white pasta—favoring instead brown basmati rice, whole-wheat pasta and rye bread. I also gave up eating potatoes— which are high on the *glycemic index*. (Never having had a sweet tooth, forgoing desserts was no sacrifice.)

Being a native of southwest France, where the positive qualities of wine and dark chocolate are readily recognized, and staying true to his roots, he encouraged their inclusion—in moderation, naturally—in his way of eating. A square of 90 percent cacao chocolate with a delicious dried fig makes a perfect finish for a meal for me now.

Following his guidelines I lost about eight pounds and stabilized my weight.

The phrase *"a way of eating"* quickly became my mantra. It helped me define an approach to my new circumstances in terms of everyday eating.

For years our diet had been centered round the Mediterranean, favoring *olive oil* as the cooking agent rather than butter.

The adjustments we made were relatively few and there was little feeling of being deprived. I say *we* as Meredith eats more or less the same way as I do. (Though when we have company, she usually makes—and eats—dessert.)

The recipes I had collected and adapted since being diagnosed in 2000 seemed suitable for a book targeted at people with type 2 diabetes.

Meredith packaged up the revised book and emailed it to our friend, Francia White, in New York who had a publisher friend, Paula Breslich in London. Paula sent it to *Constable & Robinson* whom she knew had an imprint called *Right Way* which she thought might be the place for it.

We met with them in February 2010 and they agreed. *Delicious Dishes for Diabetics—A Mediterranean Way of Eating* was published in London on August 4, 2011. It was given a new subtitle in the USA by the American publisher, Skyhorse: *Eating Well with Type 2 Diabetes*—and launched there on November 1, 2011.

From the Introduction: *This book is written for people who love food, enjoy cooking and wish to continue those pleasures despite a diagnosis of type 2 diabetes. It is also for those people who love them—because the Mediterranean way of eating is healthy for everyone.*

The book is greatly enlivened by watercolors done by a dear friend, Hope James, who spent a week watching me cook, studying the views and making household sketches that gloriously capture the beauty of the old *presbytère*. Hope has designed three kitchens for me over the years, thus providing the settings for many a happy meal.

Meredith is amused now when she walks into the kitchen to find me referring to *my own cookbook* as I prepare dinner!

And there it is—on the kitchen book shelf—tucked in among my heroes and heroines: Marcella Hazan, Elizabeth David, Nigel Slater, Sam and Sam Clark (Moro), Rose Gray and Ruth Rogers (The River Café), Ottolenghi, Claudia Roden, Jenny Baker, Jamie Oliver and Rose Elliot. (I could continue…!)

Why Does Poldark Endure?

In 2007 Sir Derek Jacobi hosted a retrospective program on PBS called *The Best of Masterpiece Theatre*—a tribute to this popular show that has been on air since 1971, showcasing the best of British costume drama.

The show producer, Darcy Corcoran, asked viewers to vote for their *12 favorite series* from the *hundreds* that have been broadcast.

Poldark came in at number SEVEN.

People evidently had *long* memories—the first series was shown in 1977 in the States. Darcy brought a small production team over to France to interview me about it some 30 *years* after it had been filmed.

The following year the BBC did a series of *reunion* programs under the umbrella title, *The Cult of Sunday Night*—revisiting series that were particularly popular with British audiences.

Poldark was one of the programs profiled.

The Cult of Sunday Night is an entertaining 30-minute look behind the scenes from a comfortable (and safe) distance. The producers managed to interview many of the surviving players—writers, directors and, of course, actors—including Angharad Rees (*Demelza*), Jill Townsend (*Elizabeth*), Norma Streader (*Verity*) and Richard Morant (*Dwight*) and me.

Richard, my running rival at the Sunday picnic long ago and the first *Dr. Enys*, was asked what *Poldark* was about and why he thought it was so successful. This was his eloquent reply:

"It's about love—it's about betrayal—the things that hurt us— the things that give us joy....Like any kind of creation where people you know are going through their emotions, expressing their feelings of love, life and death—it evokes strong attachments, strong passion—and you love it! You love them, you love the people, you cherish them, you honor them, you respect them!"

This says it all and so simply.

Dear Richard died suddenly aged 66 of an aortic aneurism in November 2011. We hadn't met for many years, but had remained in tenuous touch. He was in business designing and selling beautiful carpets manufactured in the Middle East.

He had the most life-confirming giggle of anyone I've ever met. He would say something *serious* and then after a pause, would collapse in self-deprecating laughter—though there was no doubting his sincerity.

He was coming to support the launch of my cookbook in September, but was thwarted by a huge traffic jam on the way out to Chiswick that evening—it wasn't meant to be.

I feel lucky to have known him.

In an email answering a query about *Poldark* he wrote:

"It still surprises me from emails and letters, the feeling shared that we touched so many people's hearts with our simple story, and continue to do so. I feel our world then was a much more innocent place."

The year after Richard's sudden death, dear Angharad Rees lost her long battle against pancreatic cancer, the same illness that took Ralph Bates—*George Warleggan*—back in 1991 when he was just 51 years old.

Donald Douglas, who as *Captain McNeil*, chased me (and *Demelza!*) in vain through many *Poldark* episodes has finally come to terms with the hopelessness of his pursuit and lives peacefully near us here in France. He's an excellent cook himself and the recipe for his delicious cold cucumber soup is featured in my cookbook.

*   *   *   *   *

We were filming exteriors for the second series and I remember being summoned (that's what it felt like) to the home of an elderly man in Cornwall—a gypsy "king" I was told—who had retired to a comfortable bungalow, close to the sea. He was a formidable figure sitting in his armchair in the front room. Facing him was the biggest TV I had ever seen.

"Every Sunday night you are on the screen there—like you were in the room with us," he said. "Now here you are in person. You look better on the screen!"

No answer to that—but I knew what he meant!

"The Box" sits in people's homes, everywhere—waiting benignly. Switch it on and it becomes a powerful communicator, bringing news of natural disasters, bloody battles, sporting cliffhangers and Royal weddings—daily soap operas and costume dramas—into the private intimacy of our homes. It transports us into another reality—emotionally if not quite physically.

It can make you believe in make-believe!

For many, the family saga of *Poldark* was just such a *magic carpet* and continues—apparently—to fly!

If I'd known 35 years ago, when I walked into the BBC for that first interview, what *Poldark* was going to mean to my life, I would have flunked it and lost the part.

There are aspects of *Ross Poldark* that chimed with something within me—and no acting part has ever given me greater satisfaction. "*I cherish it,*" I said in *The Cult of Poldark*—and I do.

Thanks again, Winston!! Thanks to my fellow actors—a remarkable bunch who played at full tilt and triumphed; thanks to the Beeb and to all who worked behind the scenes to make the series so memorable for so many. Thanks to *Masterpiece Theater* who brought the series to the American public across the water. And finally, thanks to the viewers around the world who continue to embrace this romantic saga.

And now, back to the kitchen to cook supper.

The New Series

At the end of May 2013 I received an email from Damien Timmer, Joint Managing Director of Mammoth Screen productions, whom I knew was preparing a completely new version of *Poldark*.

He said they would consider it a great honor to make my acquaintance and could we meet for lunch? How could I refuse such eloquence—and anyway I was intrigued to know more about what exactly they were planning.

New adaptation, new cast—obviously. How far had they got? Was the format to be roughly the same? When would they start? We arranged to meet in the restaurant at St. Pancras Station—a practical choice because Debbie Horsfield who was adapting the books for television had to return to Manchester that afternoon.

So Damien, Debbie, Karen Thrussell—the Executive Producer—and I spent an agreeable hour talking *Poldark!* They grilled me as much as I them—and they knew their stuff.

At the end of the Session I was well fed with food and info and impressed by their total commitment to the project. Their admiration and respect for Winston's books was clear, as was their determination to make it a memorable series.

The BBC had commissioned them to film *Ross Poldark* and *Demelza*—the first two books in what was now a twelve-book saga.

Damien and Karen were well on the way to persuading the Beeb to agree to a format of four hour-long episodes per book—the same as the original.

Then came the elephant-in-the-room moment. *How do you solve a problem like Robin?* Damien—who does not waste words (he writes the shortest of emails!) approached the subject with some hesitancy. The table hung on his words. After an extended moment of stop and start, he asked me what I'd like to play!

After thanking him for asking, I answered that I honestly didn't know—perhaps it would be better for Mammoth to offer something they thought appropriate. In other words, I implied that I would like to be involved—but couldn't be specific. It was, after all, 40 years since I'd looked at the books.

I emailed my thanks for lunch.

> **From:** *Robin Ellis*
> **Sent:** *Tuesday, June 11, 2013*
> **To:** *Damien Timmer*
> **Subject:** *Hello!*
>
> *Hi Damien,*
>
> *Just want to say what a delight it was to meet you and Debbie and Karen yesterday. Thank you very much for lunch and for the opportunity to get to know you all a little.*
>
> *Winston would be happy to hear that Poldark is in very safe and committed hands.*
>
> *Please let's stay in touch.*
>
> *Rxx*

It went quiet for nearly nine months! Then I wrote this blog post entitled:

March 1, 2014:
Forty Years On and Ross Poldark *remounts…*
Today the BBC announced the name of the actor who is to play the lead in the re-working of the series first screened in 1975.

Irish actor Aidan Turner has bagged it.

Congratulations to him—I hope he has as much fun as we did filming this wild and wonderful saga written in 12 books over a 60-year period by Winston Graham.

Now—two generations on—this great piece of storytelling will be enjoyed again by millions on TV and in book form.

The time is right. The wheel of fashion turns and Poldark, *an unashamedly romantic tale, can be told again with a straight face.*

The new series has the advantage of being adapted from original books written by an exceptionally gifted storyteller—Winston Graham.

The characters develop at their own pace and seem responsible for their own destiny.

No visible puppeteer, no obvious manipulation—just the telling of stories through the characters involved.

Aidan and I share a common debt to Winston, for giving us the chance to play a difficult, contrary, complex man often out of his time.

It's a roller coaster of a ride!

Then on the 28th of March 2014, I received this email:

Dear Robin,

So here are the scripts. At the very least we hope they make interesting reading. In an ideal world you'll like them—and the part—enough to want to join our Cornish escapade!

The part —The Reverend Dr. Halse—*appears in two big set pieces:*

1) Episode 4. The trial of Jim Carter. Ross *versus harsh implacable justice…in the person of* The Reverend Dr. Halse. *Chairman of the board of magistrates, mouthpiece of outraged gentry, would-be vanquisher of the underdog…until* Ross *bites back. Then…*

2) Episode 6. Ross v Halse Round Two. An extended argument over a game of cards. Again Halse has Ross on the ropes.

Two massive confrontations at key moments in the narrative. Two delicious opportunities to see you and Aidan in the same scene!

I hope you know just how much we'd like to have you on board. Ultimately it's down to whether or not the part takes your fancy.

We really hope it does.

Sincere and warmest wishes,

Karen, Damien, Debbie

I read all the scripts and found them riveting. Debbie had accomplished a brilliant reworking of the books, staying true to the original story and characters while bringing them alive for the screen with a driving energy.

I was on the line and nervous at the prospect of acting after such a gap—but there was no question, I had to say *YES!*

Again I've gone back to my blog posts to get a sense of immediacy into the story as it played out.

April 10, 2014:
Cast!
The BBC have just announced the news: Mammoth Screen have offered me a cameo in their new production of Poldark.

Reverend Dr. Halse's *day in court with* Captain Poldark.

May 12, 2014:

Friday—a long day in court!

I parked my behind on the bench at 8:30am and we wrapped at 5pm. It was the full Monty—red robe and full judicial wig—recognizable by nose alone!

I wore my minister's costume beneath—all black—which kept me warm, when all about were freezing. (Poor Meredith caught a chill and is in bed with a heavy cold!)

We were filming at Horton Court, outside Bristol, in an ancient hall dating back to Norman times made up to look like a courtroom. Beautiful, but dank and chilly, even in mid-May.

These days the shooting process is different. Forty years ago we rehearsed for six days—then spent two days in the studio preparing to record it at the end of the second day.

It was like a play—you had to know it all by heart!

"Curtain up" at 7:30pm and "down" at 10pm. Best not to be in the last scene, which was always a race against the clock.

Now you film a certain number of pages each day (in our case on Friday about four or five). There is no rehearsal.

Learn the lines and find out how best to play them on the job.

A little scary! For a while, I was thinking, "I'd rather be back in my kitchen...." Then I started to get the hang of it.

When we wrapped at 5pm, the Director, Ed Bazalgette, made a sweet remark to the assembly (many "Extras" on hand) about the unusual circumstance of having two Ross Poldarks in the same room!

Everyone clapped—which was touching.

Aidan Turner (aka Ross Poldark) and I—all smiles—relieved we'd done it—and happy we were smiling about it—shook hands warmly and vigorously.

I found myself looking forward to our next encounter in Episode 6.

August 31, 2014:
Learning the lines: Sound advice from a fellow actor—and your wife!

Ask any actor who has done time in repertory theatre what is the most frequently asked question by keen theatergoers and I'd wager the answer would be:

"How do you learn the lines?"

I might have answered "with difficulty," after drying on my first line (saying "Grace") as the Vicar *in* Murder *at the* Vicarage *on opening night at Salisbury Playhouse in the mid-sixties.*

It's the nuts and bolts of the job—but never gets any easier.

Telly Savalas as Kojak *had his lines taped all over the set and even—hard to believe—to the other actors' foreheads!*

Even if I'd been able to read them without my glasses, I couldn't be shamed into that!

Samuel West's contribution to an article in The Guardian *recently— actors' advice to fellow actors—is pertinent. To anyone learning lines for a day's filming where there is NO rehearsal, he says:*

Learn your lines with a friend the night before filming. Say them looking into your friend's eyes. Your friend will be distracting you. You will think you know the scene because you can do it looking at the floor, but human contact is distracting—and you want there to be human contact when you film the scene.

Learning the night before? I've always needed time for lines to settle and stick (slow study, it's called in the trade)—but I know what he means.

Meredith volunteered to hear my lines weeks before my first day's shoot for Poldark—*and eventually I took up her offer.*

I'd been pounding them into my reluctant brain on my daily walk for weeks.

She suggested, like Samuel West, that I aim them directly at her.

But for a while I was unwilling to engage with her spirited rendition of Captain Poldark—*and continued doing exactly what Samuel West warns against—saying the lines, very convincingly, to nowhere in particular— sometimes to the floor.*

In the end, I did engage. It was, as Sam says, usefully distracting—good preparation for when I had to project them across the chasm of the crowded, noisy courtroom.

Meredith watched the shooting of the trial of Jim Carter *(Me-lud presiding!) on a monitor in a freezing anteroom of the medieval hall where we were filming.*

In a pause while they were re-setting the lights, she popped outside for a coffee to warm herself up.

There was Aidan Turner (aka Ross Poldark*) pacing up and down, going through his lines.*

They hadn't formally met at this point. So as not distract him, she discreetly tucked herself into a corner with her coffee.

Suddenly, becoming aware that there was just the two of them, he confided: "This scene is important and I want to get it right!"

"I know it well," she said. "I rehearsed the lines over and over with Robin—playing YOU!"

Aidan roared with laughter.

Meredith sensibly didn't offer to hear his lines....

Aug 7, 2014:
Bye, Bye, Dr. Halse!

A week today at roughly 5:05 pm the Reverend Dr. Halse *walked out of the card room on the ground floor of George Warleggan's impressive mansion and disappeared. It had been a bruising encounter.*

That pest, Poldark—*more than a pest—a ruffian and a rogue—had challenged him and indeed any of his esteemed colleagues on the bench to "meet" him at any convenient time.*

An outrage.

As he headed for the door, he was heard muttering:

"He is a traitor to his class and he WILL get his come-uppance—such men are dangerous and must not be tolerated!

"Next meeting of the justices…!

"If it were up to me alone, he'd be following Jim Carter *to Bodmin Gaol or better still—the Antipodes."*

And then he was gone—in a puff of self-righteous, sulfurous smoke.

* * * * *

In truth, he popped in a unit car and with Meredith by his side was driven the short distance to the unit camp.

There he was relieved of the wig and the costume and—Jekyll and Hyde-like—resumed his everyday guise as Robin.

In a trice the car was off again, speeding towards Bath and the London train.

All that was left of the Reverend Dr. Halse *was a name on the dressing room door.*

Summing up: The series is in the can—four decades on from when the first series first aired.

My word! How the world has changed. No mobile phones then—no Internet connections—no social media—Facebooking, tweeting, Instagramming.

Techniques have changed and ways of communicating have multiplied enormously, but what has not changed for actors at all is the shared sense of joy and achievement experienced at the end of a major job well done.

There was a sweet photo of the entire *Poldark* unit on a tweet recently. It was taken soon after the shooting had wrapped. A large group of happy-looking people smiling, waving and shouting at the camera in a field somewhere near Bristol, I imagine!

There's an end-of-shoot unit photo in the printed version of this book, taken at Pebble Mill Studios in Birmingham just after the last recording had finished in 1977.

It's an indoor version, more restrained, but still showing all of us happy and relieved at what had been accomplished.

In ours, sitting in the centre of the group is Winston Graham, the man without whom none of this would have happened. We were lucky to have him with us.

Perhaps he was close by in that field, too, lending his supportive spirit to this second go-around.

Poldark has brought much joy to my life—I've often called them "*Poldark* Perks"—which doesn't do them justice.

It continues to deliver.

I am delighted to have been invited to play a role in the new venture, which has gotten off to a flying start.

Exchanging the marvelous leather coat and boots for drab, black church cloth and a sneer was tough—as was joining the Cornish establishment that *Ross* so despises, though he was born into it.

The whole experience was poignant for me and brought back many wonderful memories of 40 years ago.

Not least in my mind were my fellow members of the original cast—especially those no longer with us: the beloved Angharad Rees, Ralph Bates, Richard Morant, Frank Middlemass, Paul Curran and Mary Wimbush.

I was there for their memory—and for the late Winston Graham—as well as for the intriguing prospect of acting with the new cast to help bring this wonderful saga to a new audience.

Poldark 2015

With Mammoth Screen's Executive Producer Karen Thrussell
and Joint Managing Director Damien Timmer

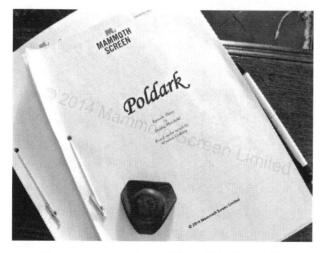

The new scripts adapted by Debbie Horsfield

Costume fitting in London at Cosprop with costumier Sion Adamson

Wig fitting on location in the make-up caravan

Awaiting my call in a freezing "green room" at Horton Court,
near Chipping Sodbury, South Gloucestershire

Donning Rev. Dr. Halse's judicial robes.
At this point I'm thinking, "I'd rather be back in my kitchen."

Preparing for the trial of *Jim Carter*—
where *Ross Poldark* and *Rev. Dr. Halse* clash. The wig is winning!

Pre-trial consultation with the Director, Ed Bazalgette

On location outside *George Warleggan*'s house
talking to the press between takes

During a break in the filming in May I had my first chance to chat
with the new *Captain Poldark*, Aidan Turner.

Sharing a joke as well as a part!

With Aidan at Horton Court

Not sure I'm a natural for the judiciary!

End of first day's shoot at Horton Court. Phew! Done it!

Aidan Turner as *Captain Ross Poldark*—scarred on the other cheek I notice!

Demelza and *Ross* (Eleanor Tomlinson and Aidan Turner)

Eleanor Tomlinson as *Demelza*

Acknowledgments

Michael Williams of Bossiney Books first published this memoir in 1977. Without his vision, it would not have been written. My thanks to him and his wife, Sonia.

Two friends—Peter Ellis [my middle brother] and Simon Perry—read the manuscript first time round; my thanks to them and to Meredith Wheeler, who read the new material and with her great good humour and love, encouraged me to go ahead.

I owe a debt to a number of other professionals in the world of publishing who have helped me, the newcomer:

My thanks to Jane Turnbull, whose "Go on, you can do it!" attitude has been a tremendous source of strength from the start. Thanks also to: Theresa Carlson Hallgarten of Octopus Books and Ken Pugh of Bookwise for their guidance and encouragement; Kate Gardener, for her enthusiasm and practical advice on the new cover; Honor Burgess for her legal good sense; and to my American connection, Johanna Baker, for helping to make the book available to *Poldark* fans in the United States.

For giving me access to their time and talent, I also thank Gerry McMahon, Mike Beatty, Robert Breckman, Joy Backhouse and Hope James.

I've enjoyed this new venture and could not have done it without their willingness to share their experience and wisdom.

This newly extended edition of *Making Poldark* has been made possible by the dedicated efforts of three women: Holly Brady of Brady New Media Publishing, who took the new edition under her wing and guided it to publication; Amy Pilkington, whose skills as a layout artist have given the book a fresh style and appearance; and my wife, Meredith, who worked tirelessly as editor and photo editor, polishing the text and making sense of the new photos.

Without their hard work, time and energy you would not be reading this book now. I raise my battered, old tricorn hat to all three and thank them very much! *Chapeau!*—as they say here in France.

I also wish to thank Andrew Graham—Winston's son—for so generously allowing us to include photos from his late father's personal album taken during the filming of the second series. These shots are a poignant reminder of Winston's enthusiastic endorsement of the BBC's *Poldark*.

—*Robin Ellis*

Photo Credits

The author and publisher would like to thank David and Charles (Holdings) Ltd for permission to quote from *The Cornish Miner* by A.K. Hamilton Jenkin. In addition, thanks to the following for lending their wonderful images to the book:

- BBC: 4, 14, 34, 52, 50, 68, 70, 78, 80, 84, 89
- Ray Bishop: 8, 36, 38, 42, 44, 80, 88
- Forbes Collins: 9, 59
- Anni Brockbank: 10, 65
- James Rusbridger: 17, 56, 82, 91
- *Birmingham Evening Mail*: 26
- Ian Barnes: 13, 57, 79
- Richard Brothers: 20
- Winston Graham: 21, 22, 32, 68, 135–143
- John Watton, Camborne School of Mines: 24
- Ken Duxbury: 25, 60
- Angus McBean: 29
- Patrick Wiseman: 49
- Joan Elliot: 66
- Christopher Cormack: 86

❧ Meredith Wheeler: 167, 168, 169, 170, 171, 172, 176

❧ Nick Kenyon: 171, 173, 174, 175

❧ Mike Hogan/Mammoth Screen: 177, 178